READING EXPLORER

FOU[R]

BECKY TARVER-CHASE • DAVID BOHLKE

Second Edition

NATIONAL GEOGRAPHIC LEARNING | CENGAGE Learning

Australia • Brazil • Japan • Korea • Mexico • Singapore • Spain • United Kingdom • United States

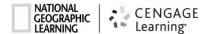

Reading Explorer Foundations
Second Edition

Becky Tarver-Chase and David Bohlke

Publisher: Andrew Robinson

Executive Editor: Sean Bermingham

Senior Development Editor: Derek Mackrell

Development Editor: Claire Tan

Assistant Editor: Melissa Pang

Director of Global Marketing: Ian Martin

Product Marketing Manager: Lindsey Miller

Senior Director of Production:
Michael Burggren

Senior Content Project Manager: Tan Jin Hock

Manufacturing Planner: Mary Beth Hennebury

Compositor: SPi Global

Cover/Text Design: Creative Director:
Christopher Roy, Art Director: Scott Baker,
Designer: Alex Dull

Cover Photo: Frans Lanting/
National Geographic Creative

Student Book with Online Workbook:
ISBN-13: 978-1-305-25450-3

Student Book:
ISBN-13: 978-1-285-84700-9

National Geographic Learning
20 Channel Center Street
Boston, MA 02210
USA

Cengage Learning is a leading provider of customized learning solutions with office locations around the globe, including Singapore, the United Kingdom, Australia, Mexico, Brazil, and Japan. Locate your local office at:
international.cengage.com/region

Cengage Learning products are represented in Canada by Nelson Education, Ltd.

Visit National Geographic Learning online at **NGL.Cengage.com**

Visit our corporate website at **www.cengage.com**

Printed in the United States
2 3 4 5 6 7 — 18 17 16 15

Contents

Scope and Sequence

Reading Skill	Vocabulary Building	Video
A: Scanning B: Skimming	A: Usage: *research* B: Usage: *solid*	Loch Ness Mystery
A: Identifying the Parts of a Passage B: Pronoun Reference	A: Word Partnership: *basic* B: Word Partnership: *painful*	A Taste of Mexico
A: Finding the Correct Definition of a Word in a Dictionary B: Understanding the Use of Commas	A: Thesaurus: *difficult* B: Word Partnership: *spend*	Right Dog for the Job
A: Identifying a Paragraph's Main Idea B: Recognizing Compound Subjects and Objects	A: Usage: *agree* B: Usage: *coast/beach*	Saving Ocean Life
A: Inferring Meaning B: Identifying the Purpose of a Paragraph	A: Word Partnership: *space* B: Word Link: *-ous*	Virus Detectives
A: Creating a Timeline of Events B: Understanding Compound Nouns	A: Usage: *village/town/city* B: Usage: *drive/ride*	Native Americans
A: Creating a Concept Map B: Understanding Compound Sentences	A: Word Partnership: *problem* B: Word Partnership: *mistake*	Parasomnia
A: Paraphrasing B: Identifying Supporting Details	A: Word Partnership: *enter* B: Word Partnership: *similar*	Penguins in Trouble
A: Understanding Complex Sentences B: Recognizing Prepositions	A: Word Partnership: *promise* B: Thesaurus: *material*	Brunelleschi's Dome
A: Identifying Text Types B: Identifying Cause and Effect	A: Word Partnership: *temperature* B: Usage: *drop vs. fall*	Storm of the Century
A: Recognizing Active and Passive Sentences B: Organizing Information in a Chart	A: Usage: *further/farther* B: Usage: *probably/definitely/possibly*	Days of the Dinosaurs
A: Supporting Ideas with Examples B: Understanding Prefixes and Suffixes	A: Word Partnership: *operate* B: Word Partnership: *future*	Deep-sea Robot

Welcome to Reading Explorer!

In this book, you'll travel the globe, explore different cultures, and discover new ways of looking at the world. You'll also become a better reader!

What's new in the Second Edition?

New and updated topics

Explore the animal world, the lives of explorers and pioneers, and amazing feats of architecture.

New Reading Skills section

Learn how to read strategically—and think critically as you read.

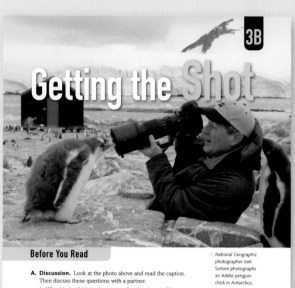

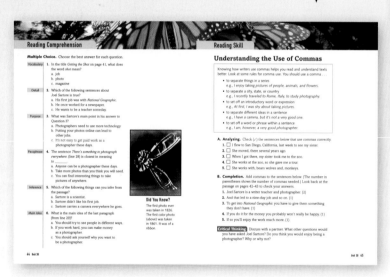

Expanded Viewing section

Apply your language skills when you watch a specially adapted National Geographic video.

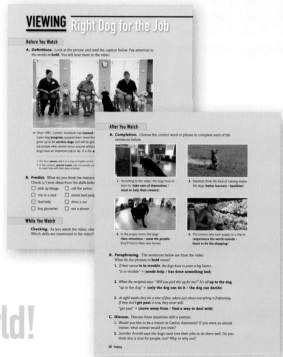

Now you're ready

to explore your world!

Mysteries

At the top of Mauna Kea, in Hawaii, a mysterious red cloud hangs above a snowy mountaintop.

Warm Up

Discuss these questions with a partner.

1. Do you think there are things that science cannot explain? If yes, give an example.

2. What do you think about when you read or hear the word *mystery*?

Sometimes **pilots** see mysterious lights in the sky. Others have seen **aircraft** that look like **disks** or "flying saucers." We call these "UFOs" (unidentified flying objects). Some people think UFOs are **alien** spaceships visiting Earth.

Before You Read

A. Definitions. Look at the photo and read the caption. Then match each word in **bold** with its definition.

1. pilots   a. machines that fly

2. aircraft   b. people who fly airplanes

3. disks   c. from other places or planets

4. alien   d. objects with a round shape

B. Skim. Quickly skim pages 9–10. What is the passage mainly about? Circle **a**, **b**, or **c**. Then read the passage to check your answer.

a. UFO sightings around the world

b. a famous place to see UFOs

c. famous movies about UFOs

Have Aliens Visited Us?

1 Many people have stories about seeing aliens. Here are two.

Judy Varns works for a group called the Mutual UFO Network. The **purpose** of this group is to **research** UFO sightings.[1] Varns thinks a place called Area 51, in Nevada in
5 the U.S., may be the best place on <u>Earth</u> to see UFOs. One day, she took some photos in the **area** and saw something she thinks is a UFO. "We saw this little disk-shaped thing in our photos. It's kind of exciting," she says.

Pat Travis lives near Area 51. One night, she saw a **strange**
10 light in the sky. The light's **movements** were very unusual. Travis saw the lights move sideways[2] and up and down. She saw them make many strange moves. Travis thinks it was a UFO.

1 When someone has a **sighting** of something unusual, they see it.

2 Moving **sideways** is moving from left to right or right to left.

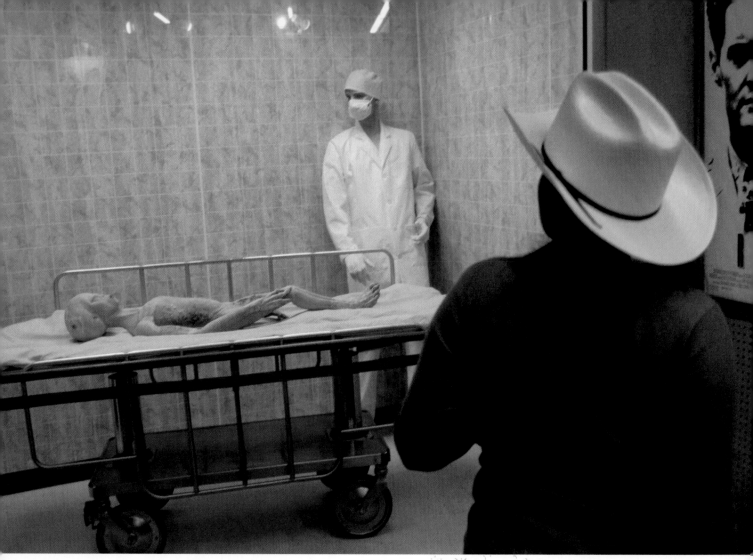

Secrets of Area 51

15 Some people think Area 51 is where the U.S. Air Force[3] keeps **secrets**, like UFOs that came to Earth and the aliens inside them. But really, Area 51 is a place the U.S. Air Force uses to test new **technology**, such as new kinds of aircraft.

    James McGaha is a pilot who flew airplanes at Area 51. "There
20 is absolutely[4] no UFO activity at Area 51," he says. "No flying saucers, no live aliens, no dead aliens."

    So what did Varns and Travis see? Bill Fox worked at Area 51, too. He thinks he knows the answer. "We did build some strange-looking airplanes," he says. "I could see why some
25 people would think they were UFOs."

    So are UFOs real? You'll have to **decide** for yourself. But if you do visit Nevada, keep your eyes on the skies!

A fake alien body lies in a display in Roswell, New Mexico, where people think an alien ship landed on Earth. Some believe the ship and aliens were taken to Area 51.

3 An **air force** is the part of an army that fights in the air.
4 **Absolutely** means "totally."

Reading Comprehension

Multiple Choice. Choose the best answer for each question.

Detail

1. Which of these sentences about Judy Varns is true?
   - a. She works at an airport in Area 51.
   - b. She helped Bill Fox build new airplanes.
   - c. She works for a group that studies UFO sightings.

Main Idea

2. What is the main idea of the second paragraph (from line 9)?
   - a. Pat Travis lives near Area 51.
   - b. Pat Travis thinks she saw a UFO.
   - c. Pat Travis has seen many unusual things.

Vocabulary

3. In line 18, the word *kinds* means _____ .
   - a. a lot
   - b. types
   - c. people

Detail

4. What was James McGaha's job at Area 51?
   - a. He flew airplanes.
   - b. He made airplanes.
   - c. He took secret photos.

Paraphrase

5. What does *"I could see why some people would think they were UFOs."* (lines 24–25) mean?
   - a. I agree with people who believe in UFOs.
   - b. I saw UFOs near Area 51 with my own eyes.
   - c. I understand why some people think they saw UFOs.

Inference

6. Which person is likely to say *"I believe UFOs are real, and could be alien spaceships."*?
   - a. Bill Fox
   - b. Judy Varns
   - c. James McGaha

Did You Know?

There is a UFO sighting somewhere on Earth every three minutes.

Scanning

You scan a text when you want to find specific information.
When you scan, you only look for the information you want.
You don't read the rest of the text. For example, for the question
Where is Area 51?, look through the text for a place name,
possibly a word beginning with a capital letter (*Nevada* or *U.S.*).

A. Scan. Look back at the passage on pages 9–10. Find and underline
these words in the passage as quickly as you can.

1. Earth   3. flew   5. dead
2. sideways   4. saucers   6. skies

B. Scan. Read the questions below. Think about what answers you
need to look for. Then scan the passage on pages 9–10, and write the
answers. Try to find the answers as quickly as you can.

1. Who works for the Mutual UFO Network? *Judy Varns.*
2. Who lives near Area 51? *Pat Travis*
3. What does the U.S. Air Force test at Area 51? *technology.*
4. What is James McGaha's job? *Pilot*
5. What did Bill Fox build? *strange-looking airplanes.*

Critical Thinking Discuss with a partner. Do you think UFOs are real?
Why or why not? What other things do you think could explain what
Judy Varns and Pat Travis saw?

A model of a
saucer-shaped aircraft,
the Couzinet Aerodyne
RC-360, built in
France, in 1952.

Vocabulary Practice

A. Matching. Read the information. Then match each word in **red** with its definition below.

Crop Circles

A farmer wakes up to find something very strange in his field. Someone or something has made strange shapes in the field by pushing down his crops.[1] The shapes can only be seen from the sky! These are called crop circles.

Where do these crop circles come from? Some people think that UFOs make the crop circles when they land. But research shows most crop circles are made by people. The technology to make them is very simple—just a rope and some wood.

What is the purpose of making crop circles? Some people make them so others will believe in aliens. Some people make crop circles just for fun. Today, some farmers even make them to mark out each different area of their farms.

1 **Crops** are plants grown in large amounts.

∧ A crop circle is made when something pushes the crops down, leaving empty spaces in the field.

1. __Strange__: hard to understand or explain
2. __purpose__: the reason you do something
3. __area__: a part of a place, or of some land
4. __technology__: the use of science and machines to do things
5. __research__: the work of trying to find facts about something

B. Words in Context. Complete each sentence with the correct answer.

1. When you **decide** what to have for lunch, you _____ what you want.
   a. don't know   b. know ✓

2. A **secret** is something you want _____ to know about.
   a. very few people ✓   b. a lot of people

3. An example of **technology** is _____.
   a. a computer ✓   b. a song

4. The **purpose** of your English textbook is to _____.
   a. have 160 pages   b. help you read better ✓

5. An example of **movement** is _____.
   a. something you hear   b. something you do ✓

> **Usage**
> **Research** can be used as a verb or a noun. *Professor Baker* **researches** *UFOs. His* **research** *will take five years.*

Before You Read

Many believe that Atlantis had rings of land with water between them. A temple stood right in the center of the island.

A. Matching. Look at the picture and read the information below. Then match each word in **bold** with its definition.

Long ago, the Greek writer Plato wrote about Atlantis—an **island** that **sank** into the sea. In his story, the people of Atlantis were very **rich**. But they were also very **greedy**. They wanted too much, so they lost everything.

1. _Sank_ : went underwater
2. _rich_ : having a lot of money
3. _island_ : land with water around it
4. _greedy_ : wanting a lot of money, things, or food

B. Scan. Quickly scan the passage on the next page. Remember that names of people and places usually start with capital letters.

1. What names of people can you find? Underline them.
2. What names of places are mentioned? Circle them.

The Lost City of ATLANTIS

1 Most people have heard the story of the **lost** island of
Atlantis. But is any part of the story true?

Over two thousand years ago, the Greek writer Plato
wrote about Atlantis, an island in the Atlantic Ocean. The
5 island's people were very rich. They built a big city with
many great buildings. At the center of the island, they
built a beautiful golden temple.[1] But the people became
greedy—they had many things, but they still wanted more.
So the gods became angry, and the island was **struck** by
10 earthquakes[2] and very large waves. **Finally**, the whole
island sank into the sea.

Many explorers have looked for Atlantis. In 2004, explorer
Robert Sarmast **reported** finding the remains[3] of a city
under the sea near Cyprus. However, Sarmast and other
15 scientists later found out the **structures** he found under
the sea were **natural**, not man-made.

Many people think Atlantis is simply a story. The
purpose of the story is to teach people not to be greedy.
Richard Ellis wrote a book about Atlantis in 1999.
20 He says "there is not a **piece** of **solid** evidence"[4] for a
real Atlantis.

So was the island real or not? We only know one thing:
The mystery of Atlantis will be with us for a long time.

---

1 A **temple** is a building where people practice a religion.

2 An **earthquake** is the shaking of the ground caused by movement of the Earth.

3 The **remains** of something are the parts that are left after most of it is gone.

4 **Evidence** is anything that makes you believe that something is true.

∧ Many people
believe very tall
waves struck the
city before it sank.

Reading Comprehension

Multiple Choice. Choose the best answer for each question.

Gist

1. Another title for this passage could be _____.
   a. Atlantis Sinks
   b. Is Atlantis Real?
   c. I Found Atlantis!

Detail

2. In Plato's story about Atlantis, the people were _____.
   a. angry at the gods
   b. wealthy but greedy
   c. greedy but beautiful

Sequence

3. What happened after Robert Sarmast said he found Atlantis?
   a. He wrote a book about his findings.
   b. Richard Ellis said that Atlantis was not real.
   c. He found out the structures were not man-made.

Main Idea

4. What is the main idea of the third paragraph (from line 12)?
   a. Scientists found out the structures were natural.
   b. Explorers found a city under the sea near Cyprus.
   c. People are looking for Atlantis, but no one has found it.

Vocabulary

5. We can replace the word *simply* (line 17) with _____.
   a. just
   b. easy
   c. sometimes

Paraphrase

6. Which sentence is closest in meaning to *"there is not a piece of solid evidence" for a real Atlantis.* (lines 20–21)?
   a. There is only one reason to believe the Atlantis story is true.
   b. The story of Atlantis is made up of many small pieces.
   c. There is nothing to make us believe the Atlantis story is true.

Did You Know?

The story of Atlantis was first written down in Plato's *Dialogues* in 360 B.C. Even today, Plato is known as one of the great thinkers of all time.

Reading Skill

Skimming

You skim a passage when you look at the whole passage quickly to see what it is about. You do not read every word. Instead, look at the title, headings, photos, and captions. Read the first line of each paragraph, and quickly read the conclusion.

A. Skim or Scan. Look at these reasons for reading. For each reason, should you skim or scan? Check (✓) the correct boxes.

	Skim	Scan
1. to see if a story is funny or serious	☐	☐
2. to find the names of countries mentioned	☐	☐
3. to find a quote (" ") by a scientist	☐	☐
4. to see if the author feels positive about the topic	☐	☐

B. Skim. Quickly skim the passage below. What is it mainly about? Circle **a**, **b**, or **c**.

a. Kimura has found Atlantis in the Pacific Ocean.
b. Kimura believes he has found a lost land near Japan.
c. Kimura has shown that the strange structures he found were made by humans.

∧ A diver explores the strange steplike structures in the waters near the Yonaguni Islands.

The Lost Continent in the Pacific Ocean

People believe that thousands of years ago, like Atlantis, the lost continent of Mu sank because of an earthquake. Today, no one knows if there really was a place called Mu, or where it was.

However, Professor Masaaki Kimura thinks he knows where the remains of Mu are. He believes they are near the Yonaguni Islands of Japan. Kimura thinks the strange structures he has found were made by people. Some other researchers don't think so. No one is sure, but the research continues.

Critical Thinking Discuss with a partner. Can you think of times you scan or skim things outside of class? What kinds of texts do you usually scan or skim?

Vocabulary Practice

A. Completion. Choose the correct words to complete the information below.

Leeds Castle, in England, has a long history. The
1. (structure / piece) of the castle is very old, and
today, it is empty—except, some say, for the ghost[1]
of a big black dog. Some believe that people who
see the dog are **2.** (struck / lost) with bad luck.

But one woman **3.** (struck / reported) that the
dog brought her very good luck. She was sitting
by a window in the castle one day. She looked
up and saw a big black dog walk through a
4. (solid / natural) wall. She got up to look for
it—and then a **5.** (piece / natural) of the window
where she was sitting fell into the water below.
Thanks to the ghost dog, the lucky woman got out
of the castle safely!

---

1 A **ghost** is the spirit of a dead person or animal.

Is there really the
ghost of a dog in
Leeds Castle?

B. Words in Context. Read the sentences and circle true (**T**) or false (**F**).

1. When an area is **struck** by a storm,   **T**   **F**
   it is suddenly hit by the storm.

2. Something that is **natural** is made by humans.   **T**   **F**

3. If something is **lost**, you know where it is.   **T**   **F**

4. When you **report** something has happened,   **T**   **F**
   you say it never happened.

5. You use the word *finally* to say something   **T**   **F**
   happened after a long time.

> **Usage**
> The word **solid** is used to
> describe objects that are fixed
> in shape and volume. **Solid**
> can also describe information
> that can be trusted.

VIEWING Loch Ness Mystery

Before You Watch

A. Definitions. Look at the picture and read the caption. Then match the words in **bold** with their definitions below.

< This photograph was **published** in London's *Daily Mail* newspaper on April 21, 1934. According to the report, the photograph was taken in Loch Ness, a famous **lake** in Scotland, where a strange **creature** is said to live. Some people are **certain** that the **monster** is real. Others are not so sure.

1. published — a. an animal of any type
2. lake — b. sure, believing completely in something
3. creature — c. an animal of strange or frightening shape or size
4. certain — d. put in a book, newspaper, magazine, or online for all to see
5. monster — e. a large body of water that is on land and not part of the sea

B. Discuss. Look at the picture again. Then discuss the questions below with a partner.

1. What do you think the picture shows?
2. Do you think it's real?

While You Watch

Checking. As you watch the video, check your answers in **Before You Watch B**. Were your ideas correct?

After You Watch

A. Sequencing. Number these events in the order they really occurred.

☐ People first reported strange movements in the lake.

☐ This photograph was published in newspapers.

☐ The Loch Ness story continued to grow.

☐ Christian Spurling told people the true story.

☐ "Duke" Wetherall took a photo of "Nessie."

☐ Newspapers in the 1930s published stories about the monster, but they had no pictures.

B. Discuss. Discuss these questions with a partner.

1. Do you believe there is a creature in Loch Ness? Why do you think so many people have reported seeing Nessie?

2. Look back at the mysteries mentioned in this unit. Which things can scientists explain? Which things can't they explain?

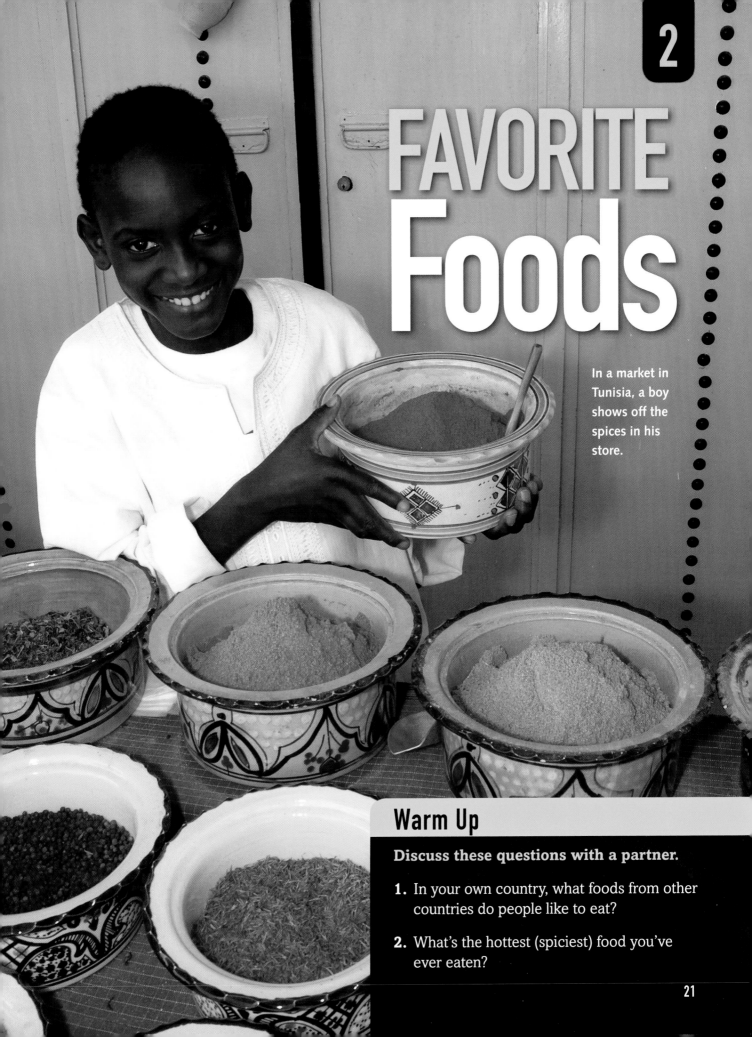

FAVORITE
Foods

2

In a market in Tunisia, a boy shows off the spices in his store.

Warm Up

Discuss these questions with a partner.

1. In your own country, what foods from other countries do people like to eat?

2. What's the hottest (spiciest) food you've ever eaten?

21

Many people believe pizzas were first made by the Greeks. Pictures like this one show the Romans made them, too. They made large, round pieces of bread and put food, olive oil, and spices on them.

Before You Read

A. Quiz. What do you know about pizza? Look at the pictures and captions on pages 22–24. Then answer the questions below.

    1. Who made the first pizza?

    2. Name some things people put on pizza.

    3. What is your favorite pizza topping?

B. Predict. Read the title and subheadings on pages 23–24. Check (✓) the questions you think the passage answers.

    ☑ Where is pizza from?

    ☐ What kind of pizza do most people like?

    ☑ When did people first put tomatoes on pizza?

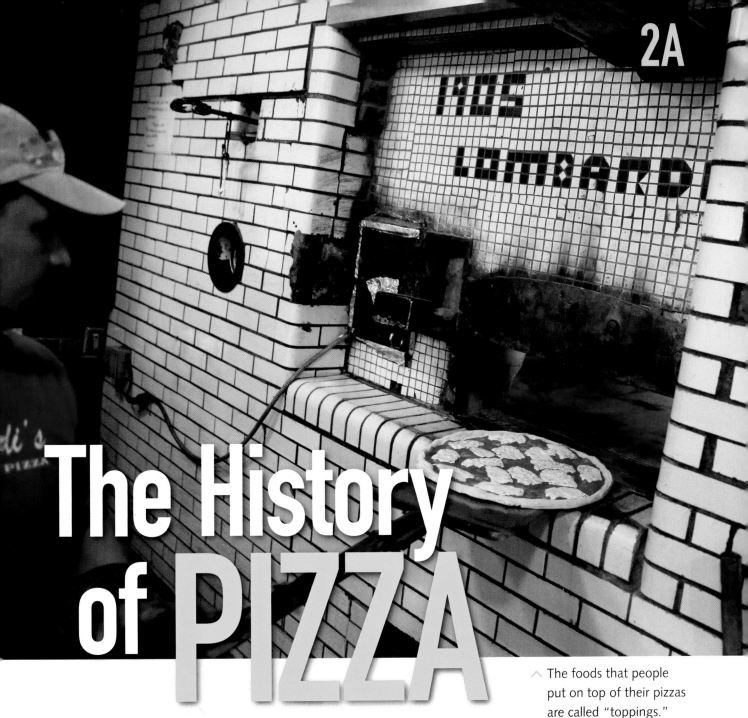

The foods that people put on top of their pizzas are called "toppings." Lombardi's, in New York City, is said to be the first pizza restaurant in the U.S.

1 Today, pizza is one of the world's favorite foods. All over the world, people make different pizzas, with different **ingredients**. But where does pizza come from? And who made the first one?

The First Pizza

5 People have been making pizza for a very long time. In the Stone Age,[1] some people mixed flour[2] with water to make dough. Then they **cooked** it on hot rocks. Over time, people started using the cooked dough as a plate, covering it with **various** other foods, herbs, and spices.[3] They had made the world's first pizza.

1 The **Stone Age** is a very early time in human history when people used things made of stone.
2 **Flour** is powder made from the seeds of wheat or corn.
3 **Herbs** and **spices** are used to add taste to food.

A New Ingredient

Then—in the early 1500s—European explorers brought the first tomatoes back from the Americas. Tomatoes are a **basic** ingredient in many pizzas today. At first, however, most Europeans thought eating tomatoes would make them sick. So, for about
15   200 years, few people ate them.

Slowly, people learned that tomatoes were safe to eat, as well as **tasty**. In the early 19th century, cooks in Naples, Italy, started the **tradition** of putting tomatoes on baking dough. The **flat** bread soon became a favorite food for **poor** people all over Naples.
20   In 1830, a cook in Naples took another big step in the history of pizza—he opened the world's first pizza restaurant.

A World Food

Today, about five billion pizzas are made every year around the world. In the U.S. alone, people eat about 350 slices every second!
25   People may not know it, but every piece is a slice of history.

Today, people across the globe can eat pizza cooked in the same way it has been for centuries.

Reading Comprehension

Multiple Choice. Choose the best answer for each question.

Main Idea

1. What is the main idea of the passage?
  a. Stone Age people made the first pizza.
  b. Pizza was an important food in Naples, in Italy.
  c. Pizza has a long history and has changed over time.

Detail

2. What does *people started using the cooked dough as a plate* (lines 7–8) mean?
  a. People put other foods on top of the dough.
  b. People cooked the pizza dough on hot rocks.
  c. People used the same pizza dough again and again.

Paraphrase

3. In lines 16–17, the phrase *safe to eat, as well as tasty* could be replaced with _____ .
  a. only safe when they tasted good
  b. safe to eat, and they tasted good
  c. good to eat if they were cooked well

Vocabulary

4. In line 17, the word *century* refers to _____ .
  a. 50 years
  b. 100 years
  c. 200 years

Detail

5. Who were the first people to put tomatoes on pizza?
  a. people in the U.S.
  b. people in Naples, Italy
  c. people in the Stone Age

Inference

6. Which of the following sentences is likely to be true?
  a. Tomatoes were a basic ingredient in pizzas in the 1700s.
  b. The first pizzas in Naples didn't cost much money.
  c. Europeans in the 1500s didn't like the taste of tomatoes.

Did You Know?

The world's largest pizza was made in Italy. It was about 40 meters (131 feet) across.

Identifying the Parts of a Passage

A reading passage can have several parts. Look at every part to get a complete understanding of the passage. This is very useful when previewing a passage or predicting what it contains. These parts include:

The **title** is a kind of **heading**. It tells you what the whole text is about.

Subheadings above **paragraphs** tell you what they are about.

The **main text** contains the most important information.

Photos and **illustrations** show information visually.

Globes and **maps** show you where in the world a place is. They also give you more visual information about a place.

Captions explain the pictures.

Footnotes give meanings for harder vocabulary words or more information.

A. Identifying. Look back at the passage on pages 23–24. Which parts of a passage are used there? Check (✓) the parts you can find.

- ☑ a title
- ☑ photos
- ☒ a globe
- ☑ subheadings
- ☒ illustrations
- ☒ a map
- ☑ a main text
- ☑ captions
- ☑ footnotes

B. Scan. Look back at the passage again, and answer the questions below.

1. How many paragraphs are there? **(3 / ⑤)**
2. How many headings are there? **(④ / 6)**
3. Does every picture have a caption? **(Y̶e̶s̶ / N̶o̶)**
4. How many footnotes are there? **(③ / 5)**
5. Is there a globe or map? **(Yes / ⓃⓄ)**

Critical Thinking Discuss with a partner. Why do you think pizza is so popular? Do you think pizza is good for you? Why or why not?

Vocabulary Practice

A. Words in Context. Complete each sentence with the correct answer.

1. If you are **poor**, you have _____ money.
   a. a lot of   b. only a little ✓

2. An example of something **flat** is _____ .
   a. a piece of paper ✓   b. a ball

3. To **cook** food, you usually make it _____ .
   a. cold   b. hot ✓

4. A **tradition** is _____ way to do something.
   a. a new ✗   b. an old ✓

5. An example of a **basic** food is _____ .
   a. bread or rice ✓   b. chocolate cake

˅ A hamburger

B. Completion. Complete the information below with words from the box. One word is extra.

> ~~cook~~ ~~flat~~ ~~ingredient~~ ~~tasty~~ traditional ~~various~~

Who Made the First Hamburger?

Around the world, there are 1. _various_ people who say the first hamburger was made in their country. For example:

Some say that in the 1200s, Mongolian soldiers had no time to 2. _cook_ their food. So they put meat under their saddles[1] to make it soft and flat, like the patties in hamburgers today.

Others in Hamburg, Germany, say hamburgers came from "Hamburg steak"—a(n) 3. _flat_ German dish. The main 4. _ingredient_ in this dish is salty meat, which is put on bread.

One story says, in 1885, a man named Charles Nagreen was selling meatballs at a U.S. fair. The meatballs were very 5. _tasty_ , but were hard to eat while walking. So Nagreen put them between pieces of bread. Without knowing it, he had made a new type of food.

Which story is true? No one knows for sure.

1 A **saddle** is a seat for a rider that is placed on a horse's back.

> **Word Partnership**
> Use **basic** with:
> (n.) basic **skills**,
> basic **needs**,
> basic **training**,
> basic **questions**.

HOT

Carolina Reaper
1.5–2 million SHU

Trinidad Moruga Scorpion
1,463,700 SHU

Naga Jolokia 1,041,427 SHU

Dorset Naga 923,000 SHU

Tabasco 190,542 SHU

Thai Chili 60,000 SHU

Jalapeño 5,500 SHU

MILD Sweet Bell Pepper 0 SHU

∧ Scientists use Scoville heat units (SHU) to rate a chili pepper's "heat" level.

Before You Read

A. True or False. Look at the information above. Then mark each sentence below as true (**T**) or false (**F**).

1. The Trinidad Moruga Scorpion is hotter than the Dorset Naga.   **T**   **F**

2. The Scoville is a type of chili pepper.   **T**   **F**

3. Tabasco peppers are hotter than jalapeños.   **T**   **F**

4. Sweet bell peppers have a very high SHU level.   **T**   **F**

B. Scan. In Assam, India, a woman named Anandita Dutta Tamuly likes to eat very hot chilies. Quickly scan the passage on the next page. Which of the chilies above is she famous for eating?

The Hottest Chilies

1 You may have **experienced** the feeling—your mouth feels like it's on fire, and the heat causes your eyes to water. You've just eaten one of nature's hottest foods—the chili pepper!

5 Chili peppers, also called chilies, are found in **dishes** around the world. They are in dishes like Indian curries, Thai tom yum soup, and Mexican enchiladas. Chilies come from the capsicum **plant**. They are "hot" because they **contain** something called *capsaicin*.

Assam, India

10 Capsaicin is very good for your health. It helps you breathe better, and it may even help keep you fit: Capsaicin makes you feel less **hungry**. It also makes your body burn more calories.[1]

We can **measure** the heat of chilies in units called Scoville
15 heat units (SHU). The world's hottest chili is the Carolina Reaper. It sometimes measures up to 2 million SHU!

Eating a hot chili can be **painful**, but some people really like to eat them. **Recently**, Anandita Dutta Tamuly, a woman from Assam, India, became famous for eating chilies. She
20 ate 51 hot peppers in just two minutes! The peppers she ate were Naga Jolokia ("Ghost Peppers"). They grow in Assam and are the third hottest chilies in the world.

"I found eating chilies was a great way to stay healthy," says Tamuly. She began eating chilies when she was a child.
25 She eats chilies when she is sick, too. "Every time I have a cold or flu, I just munch on[2] some chilies and I feel better. To be honest,[3] I barely notice them now."

∧ Anandita Dutta Tamuly eats a tray full of Naga Jolokia, "Ghost Peppers."

---

1 **Calories** are units used to measure the energy value of food.

2 If you **munch on** food, you eat it, often noisily.

3 If someone is **honest**, they tell the truth.

Reading Comprehension

Multiple Choice. Choose the best answer for each question.

Gist

1. What is the reading mainly about?
   a. how to eat very hot chili peppers
   b. interesting facts about hot chili peppers ✓
   c. ideas for cooking using chili peppers

Purpose

2. What is the purpose of the third paragraph (from line 10)?
   a. to explain why eating chilies is painful
   b. to show the effect of chilies on the mind
   c. to inform you about how chilies are good for you ✓

Detail

3. How is capsaicin good for your health?
   a. It helps you breathe better. ✓
   b. It makes you feel happier.
   c. It makes you feel hungrier.

Detail

4. How many SHUs are in the world's hottest chili pepper?
   a. up to 1,000,000
   b. up to 2,000,000 ✓
   c. up to 3,000,000

Detail

5. Which of the following sentences about Anandita Dutta Tamuly is true?
   a. She is making a movie about chilies.
   b. She uses chilies to help sick people.
   c. She started eating chilies as a child. ✓

Paraphrase

6. In line 27, the phrase *I barely notice them now* can be replaced with _____ .
   a. I usually don't eat hot chilies anymore
   b. I feel the heat of the chilies even more now
   c. I almost don't feel the heat of the chilies now ✓

Did You Know?

It's a tradition in Mexico to put chilies on Christmas trees.

Pronoun Reference

Pronouns are words such as *he, she, it, they,* and *them,* and usually refer to a noun earlier in a passage. To understand a passage, it is important to know what each pronoun refers to.

Sara bought chilies. **She** *put* **them** *in my favorite curry.* **It** *was too hot to eat!*

A. Reference. In each sentence, draw an arrow between the pronoun in **bold** and the word it refers to, as in the example above.

1. The jalapeño is a popular chili from Mexico. **It** takes its name from Jalapa, in Veracruz.

2. My brother and sister asked my mother not to put chilies in the food **she** made.

3. After Europeans brought chilies from the Americas, **they** spread very quickly around the world.

4. The cayenne pepper is hotter than the sweet bell pepper, but **it** isn't as hot as the Carolina Reaper.

5. Indians put chili peppers in many of their dishes. They often add **them** to curries.

People in the Americas were eating chilies as early as 7,500 B.C.

B. Reference. Look back at the passage on page 29. Find the following sentences in the passage, and write the word each pronoun in **bold** refers to.

1. **It** helps you breathe better. (lines 10–11) it = Capsaicin

2. She began eating chilies when **she** was a child. (line 24) she = Anandita Dutta Tamuly

3. To be honest, I barely notice **them** now. (line 27) them = chilies

Critical Thinking Discuss with a partner. What do you like or dislike about chili peppers? Why do you think Anandita Dutta Tamuly ate so many Naga Jolokia peppers?

Vocabulary Practice

A. Completion. Complete the information below with words from the box.

contains   dishes   measure   painful   recently

They may not look very tasty, but some types of cactus plants can be eaten and are very healthy. In Mexico, *nopalitos*—young stems of the cactus—have been eaten for hundreds of years.

Eating cactus has **1.** _____ become more and more popular outside of Mexico. There are many tasty and healthy **2.** _____ that use cactus stems. One easy way to cook them is in a pan, in some oil. This is how to do it.

- Clean and cut up the cactus stems. Watch out for the sharp parts of the plant! You don't want to cut yourself. That could be quite **3.** _____ .

- Next, **4.** _____ how much oil you need. Heat the oil in a pan. Add the pieces of cactus. Add some salt and cover the pan to let the cactus cook.

- The cactus **5.** _____ a strange liquid. Cook the cactus until all the liquid comes out and dries up. After that, the rest of the cactus stem can be eaten.

⌃ In a Mexican market, a man cuts and cleans cactus stems.

B. Definitions. Match the words in **red** with their definitions.

1. **plant**   •   • a. a short time ago

2. **hungry**   •   • b. having a need for food

3. **measure**   •   • c. a living thing that grows in the ground

4. **recently**   •   • d. to find out something's length, height, etc.

5. **experience** •   • e. to do or see something, or have it happen to you

> **Word Partnership**
> Use *painful* with: (*n.*) painful
> **cut**, painful **experience**, painful
> **reminder**, painful **memory**.

VIEWING A Taste of Mexico

Before You Watch

A. Definitions. Look at the picture and read the caption. Pay attention to the words in **bold**. Then match them with their definitions below.

The land around the **historic** city of Oaxaca (/wəˈhɑːkə/) in Mexico is very hard for people to move across. So, many of the native[1] **cultures** in this region— some that have **developed** for over 13,000 years—have been kept safe. This means their traditions, as well as their unique foods, are still around today. In fact, it is this **complex** mix of native traditions and cultures that makes Oaxacan food—for example, the seven types of *mole*[2] it is famous for— one of a kind.

1 If something is **native** to a place, it originally comes from there.
2 **Mole** is a kind of sauce that has chilies and often chocolate in it.

Oaxaca, Mexico

1. _____ : famous or important in history
2. _____ : grew; slowly started to exist
3. _____ : having many parts, often different from each other
4. _____ : the ideas and traditions of different groups of people

B. Predict. You will hear the following words in the video.

| traditions   dishes   ingredients   chocolate   dances   national treasures |

What do you think the video will be about? Discuss your ideas with a partner.

While You Watch

Checking. As you watch the video, check your answers in **Before You Watch B**. Were your ideas correct?

After You Watch

A. Completion. Complete the word web with words and phrases from the box.

| chilies | cooking school | Europe | history | hotel | ingredients | mole | national |

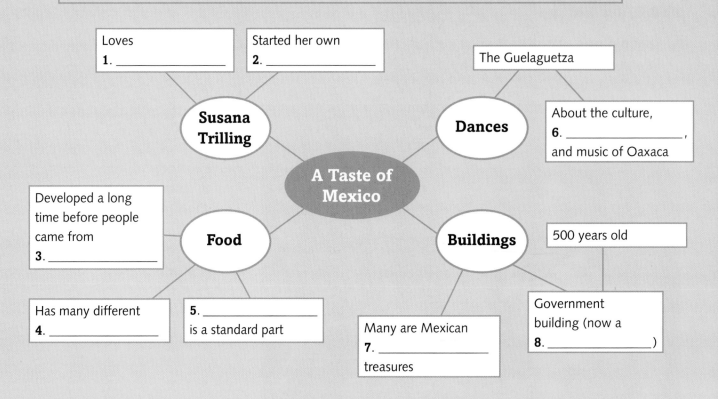

Loves
1. _____

Started her own
2. _____

The Guelaguetza

Susana Trilling

Dances

About the culture,
6. _____,
and music of Oaxaca

A Taste of Mexico

Developed a long time before people came from
3. _____

Food

Buildings

500 years old

Has many different
4. _____

5. _____
is a standard part

Many are Mexican
7. _____
treasures

Government building (now a
8. _____)

B. Discuss. Discuss these questions with a partner.

1. What traditions about food do you have in your country?
2. If you could go to a cooking school, what kind of cooking would you want to learn?

❮ A Zapotec woman makes traditional tamales. The Zapotec people are one of Oaxaca's native cultures.

Cool JOBS

Hi-tech suits keep climate scientists safe from the extreme cold as they are lowered onto the Arctic ice.

Warm Up

Discuss these questions with a partner.

1. What are the people in the photo doing? Would you like this job?

2. What interesting—or "cool"—jobs can you name? What makes them "cool"?

35

Training GRIZZLIES!

Before You Read

A. Definitions. Look at the photos and read the captions on pages 36–37. Then match each word below with its definition.

1. wrestle •   • a. a baby lion, wolf, or bear

2. paw •   • b. a person in a TV show, movie, or play

3. actor •   • c. the foot of an animal, like a dog or bear

4. cub •   • d. to teach a person or an animal

5. train •   • e. to use your body to fight someone or push them down

B. Scan. When he was 16, Russell Chadwick had an unusual summer job. Scan the first two paragraphs on page 37. Answer the questions below. Read the passage to check your answers.

1. What did Russell Chadwick do that summer?

_____

2. Where did Russell Chadwick work?

_____

Russell Chadwick copies Tank as he holds his paw up in the air.

Russell Chadwick wrestles with a little bear cub.

1 Russell Chadwick **remembers** the summer he turned 16. It was the summer he wrestled with grizzly bears!

It all started when Russell worked as an animal trainer at Wasatch Rocky Mountain Wildlife. Wasatch Wildlife is an
5 animal-training center in Utah, in the U.S. At the center, Doug and Lynne Seus train animals to be actors.

Doug and Lynne asked Russell to help **take care of** two four-month-old grizzly bear cubs named Little Bart and Honey Bump. That's more **difficult** than it sounds. Baby
10 bears are big!

Russell's job was to play with the bears. This teaches them to be **comfortable** with humans. Playing with the bears was fun, but Russell had to remember that bears are **wild** animals.

"One time, Honey Bump took a bite[1] out of my back, and I
15 had to wrestle her to the ground. But it also showed me how smart[2] she is. She knew she had done something wrong and 'apologized' by putting her head in my lap."[3]

Russell found that bears can understand more than just "sit" and "stay." For example, when Russell said "Peekaboo!" to
20 one baby bear, he **covered** his eyes with his paws, just like a human child.

Russell didn't get much money for doing this job. But he **enjoyed** the experience. He also learned a lot from it. When you've wrestled with a grizzly bear, things like work and exams
25 don't seem so difficult anymore!

1 A **bite** refers to a small piece of food, or something you grab with your teeth.
2 If someone is **smart**, they are good at learning things.
3 Your **lap** is the front area formed by your thighs when you are sitting down.

Reading Comprehension

Multiple Choice. Choose the best answer for each question.

Gist

1. What is the reading passage mainly about?
   a. how to get a summer job in Utah
   b. why wild animals make good actors
   c. what Russell Chadwick did for his summer job

Vocabulary

2. In line 1, we could change the word *turned* to _____ .
   a. became
   b. grew up
   c. went around

Detail

3. Which of these sentences about Doug and Lynne Seus is NOT true?
   a. They are movie actors.
   b. They are animal trainers.
   c. They work at Wasatch Rocky Mountain Wildlife.

Detail

4. What was the main thing that Doug and Lynne Seus wanted Russell Chadwick to do?
   a. play with the bears
   b. teach the bears to sit and stay
   c. teach the bears to live in the wild

Reference

5. In line 20, *he* refers to _____ .
   a. Doug Seus
   b. a baby bear
   c. Russell Chadwick

Main Idea

6. What is the main idea of the last paragraph (from line 22)?
   a. Tests and homework are good ways to get ready for a summer job.
   b. Russell Chadwick's experience helped him get ready for other things in his life.
   c. Russell Chadwick didn't get enough money for his summer job.

Did You Know?

When they stand on their back legs, grizzly bears can be over 2.4 meters (8 feet) tall.

Finding the Correct Definition of a Word in a Dictionary

When you look up a word in a dictionary, there is often more than one definition. To find the correct definition, first identify what part of speech the word is (e.g., noun, verb, adjective, adverb). Then look at the other words in the sentence to help you find the correct definition.

A. Matching. Identify the part of speech of the word *smart* in each sentence below. Then match each sentence to the correct definition.

1. The actor's clothes are very **smart**. _____
2. I bought a **smart**phone. _____
3. Smoke makes my eyes **smart**. _____
4. The bear is very **smart**. _____

> **smart** \ ´smaːrt \
> *adjective*
> **a.** good at learning
> **b.** fashionable
> **c.** controlled by computers
> *verb*
> **d.** to hurt

B. Completion. Circle the part of speech for each underlined word. Then look up the word in a dictionary, and write down its definition.

1. At the center, Doug and Lynne Seus train animals. (lines 5–6)
   part of speech: **noun / verb**
   definition: _____

2. That's more difficult than it sounds. (line 9)
   part of speech: **noun / verb**
   definition: _____

3. Honey Bump took a bite out of my back. (line 14)
   part of speech: **noun / adverb**
   definition: _____

4. I had to wrestle her to the ground. (lines 14–15)
   part of speech: **noun / adjective**
   definition: _____

⌃ Animal trainer Doug Seus works with Tank, a grizzly bear actor.

Critical Thinking Discuss with a partner. What animals do you think are easy to train? Would you like a summer job like Russell Chadwick's? Why or why not?

Vocabulary Practice

A. Matching. Read the information below. Then match each word in **red** with its definition.

There are many jobs that animal-lovers would be good at. For example, some people work as caregivers. Their job is to **take care of** animals. Caregivers need to feed, wash, and play with the animals they work with.

People who **enjoy** teaching animals to do tricks could become trainers. Trainers can work in a pet store, an animal park, or a zoo, but if they want to train people's pets, they have to be **comfortable** teaching the owners, too.

Some animal-lovers become veterinarians. Being an "animal doctor" can be fun sometimes. However, a vet's work is often quite **difficult**.

∧ A zoo vet holds a baby orangutan.

1. _____: not easy

2. _____: to like or have fun doing something

3. _____: okay with; relaxed

4. _____: to look after something and keep it safe

B. Words in Context. Choose the correct word or phrase to complete each sentence below.

1. If you **remember** something, you _____.
   a. think of it again   b. forget all about it

2. Examples of **wild** animals are _____.
   a. dogs and cats   b. lions and bears

3. If you **cover** something with your hands, you put your hands _____ it.
   a. under   b. over

4. Something that is **difficult** is _____ to do.
   a. hard   b. easy

5. If you **apologize**, you say that you are _____.
   a. happy   b. sorry

> **Thesaurus**
> **difficult** Also look up:
> (*adj.*) *hard, tough, challenging*

Getting the Shot

Before You Read

> National Geographic photographer Joel Sartore photographs an Adélie penguin chick in Antarctica.

A. Discussion. Look at the photo above and read the caption. Then discuss these questions with a partner.

1. What kinds of things do you usually take photos of?
2. Do you think a photographer's job is easy?

B. Skim. Skim the interview on pages 42–43. Then write each interview question above its answer in the passage.

a. I want to be a photographer. Do you have any advice for me?

b. What kind of photographers is the *National Geographic* magazine looking for?

c. Is it difficult to get a job as a photographer today?

d. How did you become a *National Geographic* photographer?

Monarch butterflies at rest completely cover a tree.

An interview with Joel Sartore

*Joel Sartore is a writer, teacher, and photographer. His words—and **images**—show his **passion** for photography and for the world around us.*

5 **Question 1:** _____

My first job was for a newspaper. After a few years there, I met a *National Geographic* photographer. He liked my photos and said I should send some to the magazine. So I did. That led to a one-day job. And that
10 led to a nine-day job, and so on.

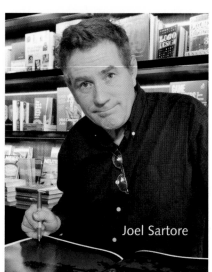

Joel Sartore

Question 2: _____

To get into *National Geographic*, you have to give them something they don't have. It's not **enough** just to be a great photographer. You also have to, for example, be
15 a scientist, or be able to dive under sea ice, or **spend** several days in a tree.

At the cutest-baby contest in Barrow, Alaska, the babies wear coats made of seal and wolf fur.

Question 3: _____

It's now more difficult to work for magazines. Technology now makes it easy to take good pictures, which means there are more
20 photos and photographers. Also, the web is full of photos from all around the world that are free, or **cost** very little. These photos are often good enough to be put in books and magazines that once **paid** for photographers and their photos.

Question 4: _____

25 Advice?[1] Well, work hard. Be passionate about every project you work on. Take lots of pictures in different **situations**. Look at others' photos thoughtfully and learn from them. And be curious[2] about life. There's something to photograph everywhere.

But be a photographer for the right reasons. If you do it for the
30 money, you **probably** won't really be happy. Do you want to make the world a better place, or make people see things in a different way? If so, you'll enjoy the work much more.

---

1 If you ask someone for **advice**, you ask them what you should do.
2 If you are **curious** about something, you want to know more about it.

Reading Comprehension

Multiple Choice. Choose the best answer for each question.

Vocabulary

1. In the title *Getting the Shot* on page 41, what does the word *shot* mean?
   a. job
   b. photo
   c. magazine

Detail

2. Which of the following sentences about Joel Sartore is true?
   a. His first job was with *National Geographic*.
   b. He once worked for a newspaper.
   c. He wants to be a teacher someday.

Purpose

3. What was Sartore's main point in his answer to Question 3?
   a. Photographers need to use more technology.
   b. Putting your photos online can lead to other jobs.
   c. It's not easy to get paid work as a photographer these days.

Paraphrase

4. The sentence *There's something to photograph everywhere.* (line 28) is closest in meaning to _____ .
   a. Anyone can be a photographer these days.
   b. Take more photos than you think you will need.
   c. You can find interesting things to take pictures of anywhere.

Inference

5. Which of the following things can you infer from the passage?
   a. Sartore is a scientist.
   b. Sartore didn't like his first job.
   c. Sartore carries a camera everywhere he goes.

Main Idea

6. What is the main idea of the last paragraph (from line 29)?
   a. You should try to see people in different ways.
   b. If you work hard, you can make money as a photographer.
   c. You should ask yourself why you want to be a photographer.

Did You Know?

The first photo ever was taken in 1826. The first color photo (above) was taken in 1861. It was of a ribbon.

Understanding the Use of Commas

Knowing how writers use commas helps you read and understand texts better. Look at some rules for comma use. You should use a comma . . .

- to separate things in a series
  e.g., *I enjoy taking pictures of people, animals, and flowers.*
- to separate a city, state, or country
  e.g., *I recently traveled to Rome, Italy, to study photography.*
- to set off an introductory word or expression
  e.g., *At first, I was shy about taking pictures.*
- to separate different ideas in a sentence
  e.g., *I have a camera, but it's not a very good one.*
- to set off a word or phrase within a sentence
  e.g., *I am, however, a very good photographer.*

A. Analyzing. Check (✓) the sentences below that use commas correctly.

1. ☐ I flew to San Diego, California, last week to see my sister.
2. ☐ She moved, there several years ago.
3. ☐ When I got there, my sister took me to the zoo.
4. ☐ She works at the zoo, so she gave me a tour.
5. ☐ She works with, bears wolves and, monkeys.

B. Completion. Add commas to the sentences below. (The number in parentheses shows the number of commas needed.) Look back at the passage on pages 42–43 to check your answers.

1. Joel Sartore is a writer teacher and photographer. (2)
2. And that led to a nine-day job and so on. (1)
3. To get into *National Geographic* you have to give them something they don't have. (1)
4. If you do it for the money you probably won't really be happy. (1)
5. If so you'll enjoy the work much more. (1)

Critical Thinking Discuss with a partner. What other questions would you have asked Joel Sartore? Do you think you would enjoy being a photographer? Why or why not?

Vocabulary Practice

A. Completion. Choose the correct words in **red** to complete the information below.

Stories Behind the Shots

Joel Sartore took this photo of an ocelot at the Omaha Zoo in Nebraska, U.S.A. Sartore **1.** (spent / paid) a lot of time with the animal, but getting the shot was not easy. "They hardly ever hold still," says Sartore. "So I really had to act quickly when he looked into my camera's lens." Many animals will stand still only long **2.** (probably / enough) to get food. After they eat enough and are not hungry anymore, the photo shoot is over.

Behind this **3.** (passion / image) is another great story. At an aquarium in Baltimore, Maryland, U.S.A., Sartore came across a very angry frog. While he tried to take a photo of it, it tried to bite him. He never thought he would be in a **4.** (situation / cost) where he was afraid of a frog! "First time for everything," says Sartore.

B. Words in Context. Read the sentences below. Then mark each sentence as true (**T**) or false (**F**).

1. Something that's **probably** true is likely to be true.   **T**   **F**

2. When you're **paid** for a photo, you get money for it.   **T**   **F**

3. If something is free, it **costs** a lot.   **T**   **F**

4. If you have **passion** for something, you like doing it very much.   **T**   **F**

5. If you have **enough** money, you don't need any more.   **T**   **F**

> **Word Partnership**
> We use **spend + time** to mean we allow time to pass when doing something (e.g., *I spent an hour at the mall.*). We use **spend + money** to mean we use money to pay for something (e.g., *I spent $100 on a new camera.*).

VIEWING Right Dog for the Job

Before You Watch

A. Definitions. Look at the picture and read the caption below. Pay attention to the words in **bold**. You will hear them in the video.

⌃ Since 1991, Canine[1] Assistants has **trained** over 1,500 dogs. In Canine Assistants' super-dog **program**, puppies learn more than just tricks. These very **smart** dogs will grow up to be **service dogs** and will be given to people who need them. The **recipients** are people who cannot move around without help or have other special needs.[2] These dogs have an important job to do. It is the **animal trainers**' job to teach them to do it.

1 The term **canine** refers to a dog or doglike animal. For example, wolves and foxes are also canines.
2 In this context, **special needs** refers to mental, emotional, or physical problems that cause some people to need help with their daily activities.

B. Predict. What do you think the trainers in the video teach the dogs to do? Check (✓) your ideas from the skills below.

- ☐ pick up things
- ☐ run in a race
- ☐ find help
- ☐ buy groceries
- ☐ call the police
- ☐ attack bad people
- ☐ drive a car
- ☐ use a phone
- ☐ turn lights on
- ☐ be comfortable with people
- ☐ perform in contests
- ☐ get along with other animals

While You Watch

Checking. As you watch the video, check your answers in **Before You Watch B**. Which skills are mentioned in the video? Are your answers correct?

After You Watch

A. Completion. Choose the correct word or phrase to complete each of the sentences below.

1. According to the video, the dogs have to learn to (**take care of themselves / want to help their owners**).

2. Scientists think this kind of training makes the dogs (**better learners / healthier**).

3. In the puppy room, the dogs (**face situations / meet the people**) they'll find in their new homes.

4. The trainers take each puppy on a trip to (**experience the world outside / learn to do the shopping**).

B. Paraphrasing. The sentences below are from the video. What do the phrases in **bold** mean?

1. *If their owner **is in trouble**, the dogs have to press a big button . . .*

   "is in trouble" = (**needs help / has done something bad**)

2. *When the recipient says: "Will you pick this up for me?" It's all **up to the dog**.*

   "up to the dog" = (**only the dog can do it / the dog can decide**)

3. *At eight weeks they hit a time of fear, where just about everything is frightening. If they don't **get past** it now, they never will.*

   "get past" = (**move away from / find a way to deal with**)

C. Discuss. Discuss these questions with a partner.

1. Would you like to be a trainer at Canine Assistants? If you were an animal trainer, what animal would you train?

2. Jennifer Arnold says the dogs must love their jobs to do them well. Do you think this is true for people, too? Why or why not?

4

Shipwrecks

A shipwreck lies half-covered by the sands of the Namib Desert in Namibia.

Warm Up

Discuss these questions with a partner.

1. Do you know about any famous shipwrecks?

2. What do you think happened to the ship in the photo?

49

Called the "Ship of Dreams," the *Titanic* was the biggest passenger ship of its time. Its makers said it was "unsinkable," but the great ship sank on its very first trip.

April 10, 1912
The *Titanic* leaves England, traveling toward New York.

April 14, 11:40 p.m.
The *Titanic* smashes into an **iceberg**.

April 15, 12:00–2:20 a.m.
Water begins to fill the ship's lower levels. **Passengers,** mostly women and children, get into small lifeboats. But there aren't enough lifeboats.

Before You Read

A. True or False. Look at the picture and read the information above. Pay attention to the words in yellow. Then mark each sentence below as true (**T**) or false (**F**).

1. An iceberg caused the *Titanic* to sink.	**T**	**F**
2. Most of the male passengers got into lifeboats.	**T**	**F**
3. Over 1,500 passengers died.	**T**	**F**
4. Nobody knew where the ship was for 100 years.	**T**	**F**

B. Scan. Read the title and the first sentence of each paragraph on pages 51–52. How many times did Robert Ballard explore the *Titanic*? Then read the whole passage to check your answer.

I've Found the TITANIC!

April 15, 2:20 a.m.
The ship breaks into two and sinks. 1,514 people die that night.

August 31, 1985 The *Titanic*'s resting place is found after 73 years. Explorers use deep-sea **submarines** to study the **shipwreck** lying on the ocean floor.

1 As a boy, Robert Ballard liked to read about shipwrecks. He read a lot about the *Titanic*. "My lifelong **dream** was to find this great ship," he says.

On August 31, 1985, Ballard's dream came true. He
5 found the wreck of the *Titanic*. The ship was in two main parts lying four kilometers (2.4 miles) under the sea. Using video cameras and an undersea robot,[1] Ballard looked around the ship. He found many **items** that told the sad story of the *Titanic*'s end. For example, he found
10 a child's shoes, a reminder[2] of the many **deaths** that happened that night in 1912.

1 A **robot** is a machine controlled by a computer.
2 A **reminder** of something makes you remember it.

In 1986, Ballard visited the *Titanic* again. This time, he **reached** the ship in a small submarine. A deep-sea robot—a "swimming eyeball"—took photos inside the ship.

15 When other people saw the photos, they wanted to visit the ship, too.

When Ballard **returned** in 2004, he found the *Titanic* in very bad **condition**. Other explorers had taken away about 6,000 items, like clothes, dishes, and shoes. Some even took pieces

20 of the ship. They think these things should be moved to a safer place, but Ballard doesn't **agree**.

Ballard believes that taking things from the *Titanic* is like robbing a grave.[3] **Instead**, he wants to put lights and cameras on and around the shipwreck. This way, people can see the

25 great shipwreck and remember what happened to it. "As long as she needs protection,"[4] says Ballard, "the *Titanic* will always be part of my life."

∧ Deep-sea explorer Robert Ballard with one of the submarines he used to explore the *Titanic*

3 **Robbing a grave** is taking things from where a dead body is kept.

4 If someone gives you **protection**, they keep you safe from danger.

"As long as she needs protection, the *Titanic* will always be part of my life."

— Robert Ballard

Lights from a submarine break the darkness of the deep sea to show the bow (the front) of the *Titanic*.

Reading Comprehension

Multiple Choice. Choose the best answer for each question.

Gist

1. What is the reading mainly about?
   a. how visitors to the *Titanic* leave it in bad condition
   b. Robert Ballard's hopes that more people will visit the *Titanic*
   c. how Robert Ballard found the *Titanic* and wants to keep it safe

Detail

2. The first time he explored the *Titanic*, Ballard did NOT _____.
   a. take photos inside the shipwreck
   b. find a child's shoes in the shipwreck
   c. use a robot to look around the shipwreck

Detail

3. Which of the following sentences about Ballard is true?
   a. He read about the *Titanic* when he was a child.
   b. He swam into the *Titanic* wreck to take photos.
   c. On his second trip to the *Titanic*, he found the ship in bad condition.

Detail

4. According to the passage, what did people see that made them want to visit the *Titanic*?
   a. the submarine Ballard used
   b. photos from inside the ship
   c. items that were taken from the ship

Reference

5. Who does *they* refer to in line 20?
   a. Robert Ballard and his team
   b. other visitors to the *Titanic* shipwreck
   c. people from the *Titanic* who are still alive

Inference

6. Which statement would Ballard probably agree with?
   a. People should not remove anything from the *Titanic*.
   b. Lights and cameras will hurt the remains of the *Titanic*.
   c. The *Titanic* wreck should be moved out of the water completely.

Did You Know?

Each lifeboat on the *Titanic* could hold 65 people. Sadly, when the ship sank, many lifeboats were not full. One boat, for example, only had 35 people in it.

Identifying a Paragraph's Main Idea

The main idea of a paragraph is its central idea. To determine the main idea, skim the paragraph and ask yourself, "What point is the author trying to make?" The first and last sentences of a paragraph, as well as its heading (if it has one), can also give you clues about the main idea.

A. Multiple Choice. What is the main idea of the text below? Circle **a**, **b**, or **c**.

a. The *Carpathia* took over three hours to get to the *Titanic*.

b. The *Carpathia* answered the *Titanic*'s call and helped save lives.

c. The *Carpathia* was too far away to help stop the *Titanic* from sinking.

On April 15, 1912, at 12:20 a.m., the British ship *Carpathia* got a message from the *Titanic*. The "Ship of Dreams" was sinking. The *Carpathia* was 93 kilometers (58 miles) away. It traveled at top speed to where the *Titanic* was, even though there were dangerous icebergs in the ocean. It arrived at 3:30 a.m., over an hour after the *Titanic* sank. Still, the *Carpathia* was able to pick up 711 people. The ship then went to New York, arriving there on April 18.

B. Matching. Look back at the passage on pages 51–52. What is the main idea of each paragraph?

Paragraph 1: a. Ballard read a lot about the *Titanic*.
            b. Ballard's dream was to find the *Titanic*.

Paragraph 2: a. Ballard found items like a child's shoe.
            b. Ballard finally found the shipwreck he was looking for.

Paragraph 3: a. Ballard reached the ship in a small submarine.
            b. Ballard returned and took photos of the ship.

Paragraph 4: a. Other explorers had taken things from the *Titanic* wreck.
            b. Ballard thinks taking items from the ship hurts the wreck.

Paragraph 5: a. Ballard wants to protect the *Titanic*.
            b. Ballard wants to put lights and cameras around the ship.

Critical Thinking Discuss with a partner. Robert Ballard thinks no one should take things from the *Titanic*. Do you agree with him?

A. Completion. Complete the information using words from the box. One word is extra.

conditions	deaths	items	reach	returned

Why were there so many **1.** _____ on the night the *Titanic* sank? One reason is that the **2.** _____ in which people waited to be saved were very bad. The air and water were very cold. Scientists believe most of the people who fell into the water died from the cold in less than 15 minutes. However, the main reason is that there were not enough lifeboats. There were 2,223 people on the ship, but lifeboats for only 1,186 people. Also, many people could not **3.** _____ the boats before the ship sank. In the end, only 705 people **4.** _____ safely to land.

^ At first, most people could not believe the news of the *Titanic*'s sinking.

B. Words in Context. Complete each sentence with the correct answer.

1. If people **agree**, they have _____ about a subject.
  a. the same idea   b. different ideas

2. If you drink tea **instead of** coffee, you drink _____.
  a. tea   b. both tea and coffee

3. An example of an **item** of clothing is _____.
  a. warmth   b. a jacket

4. A lifelong **dream** is something you have _____ all your life.
  a. wanted to do   b. tried to stop doing

5. If you **reach** a place, you are _____ get there.
  a. able to   b. not able to

6. If you **return** to somewhere, you go there _____.
  a. for the first time   b. again

Usage
If you **agree with** someone, you have the same idea or opinion as that person.
If you **agree to** do something, you say that you will do it.

Treasure Ship

Before You Read

A. Matching. Look at the picture and read the caption.
Match each word in **bold** with its definition.

1. _____: land next to the sea
2. _____: people who work on a ship
3. _____: hard pieces inside a body that give it shape
4. _____: the shape that all the bones in your body make

B. Predict. Read the first sentence of each paragraph on the next page.
Check (✓) the information you think you'll read about. Then read the
passage to check your answers.

☐ how a ship became wrecked

☐ what was found on the shipwreck

☐ maps that show where the ship is

☐ a fight over gold coins

⌃ In the 1500s, the fastest
way to travel from Europe
to India was to pass the
coast of southern Africa.
But **sailors** feared this
area, named **Skeleton**
Coast for the many animal
bones found there. It is
now famous for its large
number of shipwrecks.

1　*On a **beach** along the Skeleton Coast, the sand is filled with diamonds. But in April 2008, workers found something very different: a piece of lost history—a shipwreck and its treasure.[1]*

The story began when a worker from the nearby diamond mines
5　found a piece of **metal** on the beach. It was a piece of copper. Soon, they found more copper and many gold coins.[2] The workers then found that these came from the remains of a large ship. The shipwreck was the real treasure.

Archeologists[3] studied the shipwreck. They thought the ship
10　probably came from Portugal about 500 years before. However, it was difficult to find information about it. In 1775, many maps and books about the ships of the time were lost in a fire in Lisbon. "That left a big **hole** in our history," says Portuguese archeologist Alexandre Monteiro.

15　Finally, Monteiro found out that a group of ships left Lisbon for India in 1533. One of them, the *Bom Jesus*, **carried** 300 people and a large **amount** of treasure. The Portuguese sailors planned to use the treasure to buy **expensive** Indian spices. Archeologists now believe the wreck might be the *Bom Jesus*. This is because
20　many of the gold coins found were Spanish. Monteiro found an old **letter** in the Spanish royal archives.[4] The letter said that Spain gave Portugal money for the trip. Two thousand Spanish coins were put on the *Bom Jesus*. This could explain why so many Spanish coins were found in a Portuguese shipwreck.

25　So what happened to the ship? The *Bom Jesus* probably got lost in a storm. Then it smashed into rocks near the coast and sank. There were few human bones found, so the sailors were probably able to get off the ship. But even if they swam onto the beach, they would have found themselves in a strange, **distant** land.
30　They had no way to get home. They might as well have been on Mars. To this day, no one knows what happened to them.

∧ Part of the treasure of the *Bom Jesus*. Almost 23 kilograms (50 pounds) of gold coins were found in the sand.

The Skeleton Coast

1　**Treasure** is something expensive and hard to find.

2　A **coin** is a small piece of metal used as money.

3　An **archeologist** studies old things, to find out about the past.

4　The term **royal archives** refers to a place where old papers, etc., owned by the king are kept.

Reading Comprehension

Multiple Choice. Choose the best answer for each question.

Detail

1. What did the worker first find on the beach?
   a. a diamond
   b. a piece of gold
   c. a piece of copper

Paraphrase

2. Which sentence is closest in meaning to *The shipwreck was the real treasure.* (line 8)?
   a. There were a lot of expensive items on the ship.
   b. The shipwreck was a very important discovery.
   c. The coins on the ship weren't real, but it was an important ship.

Purpose

3. What is the purpose of the third paragraph (from line 9)?
   a. to describe how a fire destroyed a part of the ship
   b. to describe what books and maps were like in the 1500s
   c. to explain why it's difficult to know much about the ship

Detail

4. What is NOT true about the *Bom Jesus*?
   a. It was a Portuguese ship.
   b. It was returning from India.
   c. It was carrying Spanish money.

Fact or Theory

5. Which statement is a fact?
   a. All the sailors were able to swim to land.
   b. There were 2,000 Spanish coins on the *Bom Jesus*.
   c. The ship got lost in a storm and smashed into rocks.

Inference

6. Why does the author say the sailors *might as well have been on Mars.* (lines 30–31)?
   a. to show how bad the sailors' situation was
   b. to compare the Skeleton Coast to what Mars looks like
   c. to say that the sailors had found a beautiful but strange place

Did You Know?

There are over a thousand shipwrecks on the Skeleton Coast.

Recognizing Compound Subjects and Objects

A sentence can have a single subject or a compound subject. A compound subject is a subject that contains two or more nouns. Sentences can also contain compound objects. Look at the examples below.

Compound subject: (_Ballard_ and _his team_) _found the_ Titanic _in 1985._

Compound object: _Ballard used_ (_cameras_ and _a robot_) _to look at the ship._

A. Analyzing. Find and circle examples of compound subjects and objects in the passage below. In each example, underline the different subjects or objects.

> On July 17, 1956, the _Andrea Doria_ left Italy for New York. The ship was carrying over 1,700 passengers and crew members. A week later, the _Stockholm_ left New York for Sweden. That night, the _Andrea Doria_ and _Stockholm_ crossed paths with tragic results. Just after 11:00 p.m., the _Stockholm_ smashed into the side of the _Andrea Doria_. The _Andrea Doria_ began to slowly sink. The _Stockholm_ helped with the rescue of the passengers, but there would be 52 deaths that night. Were darkness and bad weather the cause of the accident? It remains a mystery to this day.

∧ The _Andrea Doria_ and the _Stockholm_ crash into each other in the North Atlantic Ocean.

B. Scan. Find examples of compound subjects and objects in the passage on page 57. Fill in the blanks.

1. Compound object: _____ and _____ (paragraph 2)
2. Compound subject: _____ and _____ (paragraph 3)
3. Compound object: _____ and _____ (paragraph 4)

Critical Thinking Discuss with a partner. What do you think should happen to the treasure from ships like the _Bom Jesus_? Should the people who find it get to keep it? Why or why not?

Vocabulary Practice

A. Definitions. Read the information. Then complete the sentences below with the correct form of the words in **red**.

Silver Shipwreck

On August 2, 2013, a company called Odyssey Marine Exploration removed over 50,000 kilograms (120,000 pounds) of silver from a shipwreck off the coast of Ireland—the heaviest **amount** of the **metal** ever taken from a shipwreck. The ship, the *S.S. Gairsoppa,* was **carrying** tea, iron, and silver from the **distant** lands of India, when it sank in 1941. Today, that much silver is worth almost $75 million. In addition to the silver, the company also found some newspapers and **letters** written by the sailors.

Silver from the *S.S. Gairsoppa*

1. If you are _____ something, you are moving it somewhere.

2. The _____ of something is how much of it there is.

3. Something that is _____ is very far away in space and time.

4. Silver and gold are two types of _____ .

5. A(n) _____ is a written message from someone, usually sent by mail.

B. Completion. Complete each sentence with a word from the box. One word is extra.

> beach   distant   expensive   hole   metals

1. After the ship ran into the rocks, a big _____ in its side let in water.

2. The ship sank quickly. Only one man was able to reach a(n) _____ and live to tell the story.

3. Many older ships carried a lot of silver and gold coins. More recent ships carry heavy bars of these _____ .

4. Searching for shipwrecks can be _____ . Some people can spend millions of dollars looking for a wreck.

Usage
Coast refers to a piece of land along or near the ocean, while **beach** refers to a piece of land near a large body of water that is filled with sand or small stones.

VIEWING Saving Ocean Life

Before You Watch

A. Definitions. Look at the picture and read the caption. Pay attention to the words in **bold**. You will hear them in the video. Match the words with their definitions below.

∧ Trawling is a way of fishing in which giant **nets** with heavy **weights** are put into the ocean. These nets are pulled along the **bottom** of the ocean, so the fish can't get away. Many fishermen[1] like trawling because they can bring in a lot of fish at a time. However, the nets and the weights **scrape** up everything on the ocean floor, and a lot of plants and animals that the fishermen don't need are hurt, too. Today, experts are trying to find ways to **protect** ocean life from trawling ships. One of these ways is to sink an old ship, and leave the shipwreck on the ocean floor.

> 1 **Fishermen** are people who make money by fishing.

1. nets •   • a. to keep safe
2. weights •   • b. the lowest part
3. bottom •   • c. heavy things used to hold something down
4. scrape •   • d. pieces of cloth, string, etc., tied together to hold things
5. protect •   • e. to remove a layer off something by moving something rough or sharp across it

B. Predict. How do you think a shipwreck can help save ocean life? Discuss your ideas with a partner.

While You Watch

Checking. As you watch the video, check your answers in **Before You Watch B**. Were your ideas correct?

After You Watch

A. Completion. Choose the correct word or phrase to complete each sentence below.

1. This shipwreck was once a (**war / passenger**) ship.

2. The shipwreck protects ocean life by (**tearing up trawl nets / damaging the trawler ships**).

3. Before they sink an old ship, workers take off all the (**metal / wood**).

4. After a few years, the shipwreck (**moves to a new place / falls apart**).

5. According to the video, another way to protect the ocean floor may be to (**build concrete walls / grow more sea plants**).

6. Sobel believes people are (**smart / scared**), so they'll do the right thing to protect the ocean.

B. Discuss. Discuss these questions with a partner.

1. Jack Sobel says, "I'm an optimist. I think we'll be successful." What do you think he means?

2. What other ways can we protect ocean life? Are there things you can do to help?

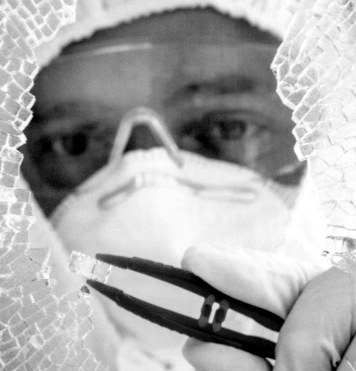

5

Science INVESTIGATORS

An investigator looks at a piece of broken glass. Crime scene investigators are scientists who work with the police.

Warm Up

Discuss these questions with a partner.

1. What do you think the investigator in the photo is looking for?

2. What kinds of people, besides crime scene investigators, use science in their jobs?

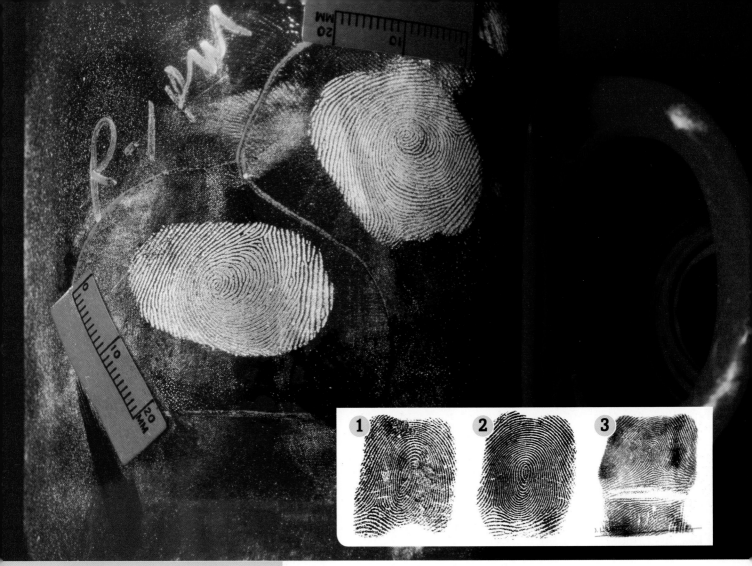

Before You Read

When there's a crime,[1] the police often call a **crime scene investigator**. This person helps the police study the **scene**, looking for evidence.[2] One thing they look for is **fingerprints**. Everyone has a different **pattern** of fingerprints.

A. Discussion. Look at the pictures and information above. Pay attention to the words in **bold**. Then answer the questions.

1. Who do crime scene investigators help?
2. Besides fingerprints, what else do you think a crime scene investigator could look for?
3. Look at your own fingers. What patterns can you find?

B. Scan. Quickly scan the passage on pages 65–66. Underline all the clues the crime scene investigator finds.

1 The lines on this fingerprint form patterns that are called **loops**.

2 These lines form around a single point. These are called **whorls**.

3 The lines here form **arches**. Many people have this pattern.

---

1 A **crime** happens when someone does something bad, or breaks the law.

2 **Evidence** refers to things that can help the police find out who did the crime.

At the Scene of a Crime

1 Your phone rings. The police officer says someone broke into[1] a store and took some expensive items. They need you right away. It is your job to study the whole scene for **clues** that will help **catch** the thief.[2] You are a crime scene investigator,
5 and the game is on.

Outside the store, you see a broken window, some glass on the street, shoeprints, and marks made by a **vehicle's** tires.[3] You look at the shoeprints. They're large, so you're likely looking for a man. You photograph the shoe's pattern. This
10 can tell you the type of shoe. You then measure the **space** between the shoeprints. You now know how long the man's **steps** were. This gives you an idea of how tall he was.

As you follow the shoeprints over to the tire marks, they get farther away from each other. They lead to the passenger's
15 side of the vehicle. Now you know the man probably didn't work alone. You photograph the tire marks. They can help you find out what type of vehicle it was, and the **direction** it went in.

A crime scene investigator begins looking for fingerprints in places the thief is likely to have touched, like the front door.

1 If someone **breaks into** a place, they go inside though they are not allowed to be there.

2 A **thief** is someone who takes something that they do not own.

3 A **tire** is the outside of a car wheel. It is usually black and made of rubber.

The print left by a shoe can say a lot about the person wearing it. So at a crime scene, the print is measured. Then it is studied under colored light that makes the pattern clearer.

On the Case

20 The most important clues will come from a person's body. The person who broke in left a little of himself behind. In the store, you find some fingerprints. Using a computer, you can **compare** these prints against millions of others.

In the store, there is a lot more glass. Then you find something
25 else—a hair. You keep this because you know hair contains a person's DNA.[4] You can compare this with other people's DNA, too. If you find a match for the fingerprint or the DNA, you will know who was in the store.

Will you find the thief? You now have a lot of information, so it's
30 **possible**. For a crime scene investigator, it's all in a day's work.

---

4 A person's **DNA** contains information about that person. It tells a person's body things like what color its eyes or hair should be.

Reading Comprehension

Multiple Choice. Choose the best answer for each question.

Gist

1. What is this reading mainly about?
   a. how an investigator used clues to find a famous thief
   b. what a crime scene investigator finds at a crime scene
   c. how thieves are using new technology to break into places

Vocabulary

2. What can the word *likely* in line 8 be replaced with?
   a. carefully
   b. probably
   c. comfortably

Detail

3. In the passage, why was the investigator interested in a shoeprint?
   a. because it had a very strange pattern
   b. because it showed how tall the thief was
   c. because it showed the direction the thief went

Detail

4. Which of the following do the tire marks NOT show?
   a. the direction the thief went
   b. how heavy the thief's car was
   c. the type of car the thief used

Detail

5. What are the most important clues that the investigator finds?
   a. fingerprints and a hair
   b. shoeprints and tire marks
   c. video from the store's camera

Inference

6. How would the author probably answer the question, "Will the thief be caught?"
   a. Yes, he will.
   b. Maybe.
   c. I don't think so.

koala   human

Did You Know?

A koala's fingerprints look just like a person's fingerprints.

Reading Skill

Inferring Meaning

A text does not always state everything directly. Sometimes you need to infer meaning by "reading between the lines." You can infer meaning by using what you already know about the topic, clues in the text, and common sense. For example, in the passage on pages 65–66, we know the shoeprints were large, so it is likely that they were a man's.

A. Inference. Look at some facts from the passage on pages 65–66. What can you infer?

1. There was more broken glass inside the store than outside.
   a. The thief broke the window from the inside.
   b. The thief broke the window from the outside.

2. The space between shoeprints near the tire marks got farther apart.
   a. The thief was walking slower, and then stopping.
   b. The thief was walking faster, maybe running.

3. The shoeprints led to the passenger's side of the car.
   a. The thief drove the car.
   b. Someone else drove the car.

B. Inference. How sure are you of these things? Check (✓) the things you can infer from the passage.

1. ☐ The crime happened at night.
2. ☐ Some things were missing from the store.
3. ☐ The fingerprints belong to the thief.
4. ☐ The hair belongs to the thief.
5. ☐ The investigator will look for a match for the fingerprints.
6. ☐ The investigator will find a match for the fingerprints.

Critical Thinking Discuss with a partner. Can the information from fingerprints and DNA ever be wrong?

∧ A burglar breaks a window while breaking into someone's house.

Vocabulary Practice

A. Completion. Choose the correct words to complete the information below.

We know that one of the best ways to **1.** (**catch** / **step**) a thief is by collecting fingerprints from a crime scene and then **2.** (**comparing** / **stepping**) them to others with a computer. But how difficult is it to get the prints?

Powder covers the pattern of the fingerprint, so it can be seen clearly.

Try this: Press a finger onto a drinking glass. If your fingers are oily or wet, the print will be better. Then cover the print with a small amount of powder. You can use things you have in your kitchen, such as flour or cocoa powder.

Now remove some of the powder with a small, dry paintbrush. Go in a circular **3.** (**direction** / **space**) until you see the print. Then place some tape over the print. Take the tape off and put it on a piece of paper. If **4.** (**catching** / **possible**), use colored paper. You should now see the fingerprint clearly.

B. Words in Context. Choose the best answer for each question below.

1. In which of these situations would a **clue** be helpful?
   a. when doing a puzzle   b. when building a house

2. Which of these do you use to take a **step**?
   a. your hands   b. your feet

3. Which of these things is an example of a **vehicle**?
   a. a house   b. a bus

4. Which of these things has more **space**?
   a. a large room   b. a box filled with books

> **Word Partnership**
> Use *space* with: (*adj.*) **open** space, **empty** space, **office** space, **living** space, **public** space.

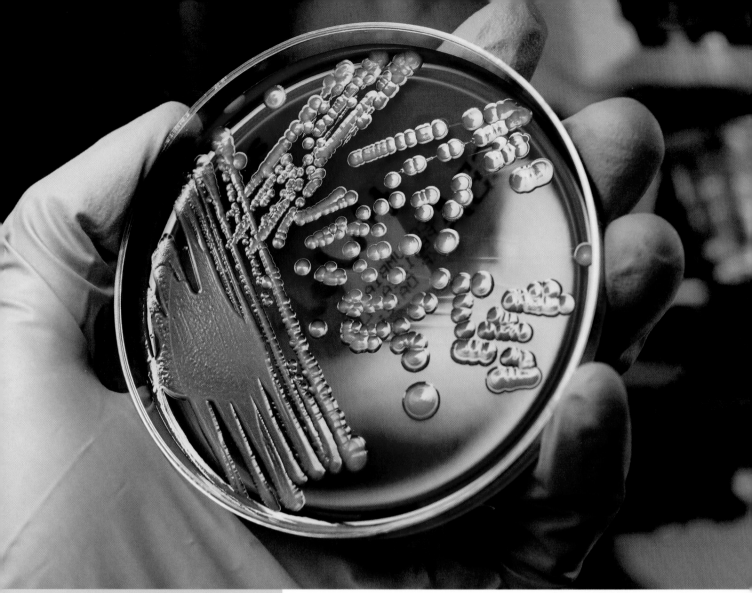

Before You Read

A. Matching. Look at the photo and read the caption. Then match each word in **bold** with its definition.

1. _____: kinds or groups of bacteria

2. _____: sick

3. _____: a kind of very small living thing

4. _____: a machine that shows a larger view of something very small

B. Predict. Look quickly at the photos and headings on page 71. Check (✓) the information you think you'll read about. Then read the passage to check your answers.

☐ how a doctor found the cause of an illness

☐ how *E. coli* has caused many deaths around the world

☐ how more people want to become doctors

△ **Bacteria** are so small, you need a **microscope** to see them. *E. coli* is a type of bacteria that can be found in both animals and humans. Many **strains** of *E. coli* won't hurt you, but some can make you very **ill** or cause death.

The Disease Detective

1 Six children were in the hospital. They were very sick, but the doctors didn't know what to do. They called Dr. Richard Besser, an **expert** on strange illnesses.[1] Dr. Besser knew just what to do.

Finding a Cause

5 First, Dr. Besser needed to find the cause of the illness. He used a microscope to look for **germs** like bacteria in the children's bodies. Dr. Besser found that all the children had a strain of the bacteria *E. coli*. Then he looked at the bacteria's DNA. The DNA showed him that this strain of *E. coli* was **dangerous** to humans.

Where Did It Come From?

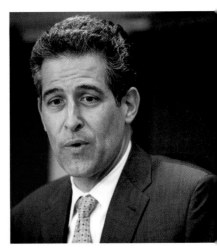

∧ Dr. Richard Besser is an expert on illnesses that move and kill quickly.

10 Dr. Besser knew *E. coli* could move from animals to humans. **Perhaps** the children had **touched** animals that carried the bacteria? Besser found other *E. coli* cases in the area where the children lived. But it wasn't enough.

15 Besser then made a **list** of what the sick children had eaten. They had all eaten cheese, apple juice, and fish. He then made a list of what healthy children in the area had eaten, and compared his lists. They had eaten the cheese and fish, but not the apple juice.

Case Closed

20 Besser went to where the apple juice was made. He saw that there were animals around the apple trees, and he saw the workers using **dirty** apples that had fallen on the ground. More importantly, he saw that the apples were not washed before the juice was made, and that the juice was not heated. Doing these things would **kill**
25 the bacteria. Besser then knew it was the apple juice that made the children sick.

Besser's *E. coli* case has a happy ending. The children got better. And what Besser learned that day now helps keep others safe.

---

1 A **disease** or an **illness** is something that makes you sick.

Reading Comprehension

Multiple Choice. Choose the best answer for each question.

Gist

1. Another title for this passage could be _____.
a. Good vs. Bad Bacteria
b. Looking for Answers
c. A Death at the Hospital

Sequence

2. Which of the following things happened first?
a. Dr. Besser found out what made the children sick.
b. Dr. Besser made a list of what the sick children ate.
c. Dr. Besser went to where the apple juice was made.

Detail

3. Which of the following is NOT true about *E. coli*?
a. It's a kind of plant.
b. It can make people sick.
c. It moves from animals to people.

Reference

4. Who does *they* refer to in line 18?
a. the sick children
b. the healthy children
c. both the sick and the healthy children

Cause and Effect

5. What made the children sick?
a. old fish
b. dirty apples
c. smelly cheese

Inference

6. What advice would Dr. Besser probably agree with?
a. Never drink apple juice from a supermarket. You should make it yourself.
b. Stay away from animals that live near trees. They will make you sick.
c. Don't eat fruit from the ground. Wash the fruit before you eat it.

Did You Know?

There are about two kilograms (four pounds) of bacteria in a human body.

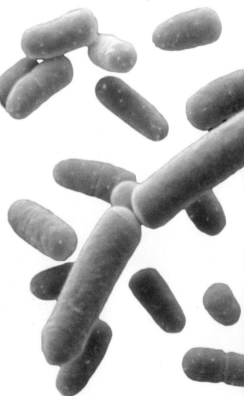

Identifying the Purpose of a Paragraph

Identifying a paragraph's purpose (or purposes) helps you understand the organization of a passage. The first line of a paragraph and its heading (if it has one) can give you clues about its purpose. These purposes can include:

- to introduce a topic
- to answer a question
- to give an example
- to describe a solution

- to continue a point
- to give data and statistics
- to make an argument
- to summarize ideas

A. Identifying Purpose. Look back at the photo and caption on page 70. Check (✓) the purpose(s) of the information in the caption.

- ☐ to introduce a topic
- ☐ to give statistics
- ☐ to help explain a photo
- ☐ to ask a question
- ☐ to give a definition
- ☐ to provide facts

B. Identifying Purpose. Look back at the passage on page 71. What is the main purpose of each paragraph?

1. **Paragraph 1**
   a. to give background information
   b. to summarize what will come later

2. **Paragraph 4**
   a. to list a sequence of actions
   b. to answer a question

3. **Paragraph 5**
   a. to introduce a new topic
   b. to answer a question

4. **Paragraph 6**
   a. to describe the end of an event
   b. to predict what will happen

⌄ A good way to keep safe from germs is to wash your hands often.

Critical Thinking Discuss with a partner. How do you think we can keep safe from germs?

Vocabulary Practice

A. Completion. Complete the information below with the correct form of words in the box. One word is extra.

dangerous	dirty	expert	kill	touch

When a bee stings a person, the bee's "poison"[1] goes into their body. To most people, a bee sting is painful, but it's not really **1.** _____. However, for some, a little bee sting can **2.** _____. In fact, every year, there are many people who die from bee stings.

But scientists are learning that bee stings can also be used to help people. Dr. Chris Kleronomos is a(n) **3.** _____ on natural medicines. He is trying to help a young man named Erick. Erick has a disease that causes his muscles to hurt. He experiences a lot of pain when people **4.** _____ him. Dr. Kleronomos uses the bee's poison to take away Erick's pain. It may sound strange, but for people like Erick, it seems to be working.

---

1 A **poison** is something that causes illness or death if you eat or drink it.

B. Words in Context. Read the sentences below. Mark each sentence as true (**T**) or false (**F**).

1. In a restaurant, most people are happy to eat off a **dirty** plate.   **T**   **F**

2. **Perhaps** is another way to say *maybe* or *possibly*.   **T**   **F**

3. A **list** usually has just one thing on it.   **T**   **F**

4. An **expert** on a subject knows a lot about it.   **T**   **F**

5. **Germs** can make people sick.   **T**   **F**

Word Link

The suffix **-ous** (meaning "full of") can be added to some nouns to make adjectives. For example: *danger* → *dangerous*, *mystery* → *mysterious*, *adventure* → *adventurous*.

VIEWING Virus Detectives

Before You Watch

A. Definitions. Look at the picture and read the caption. Pay attention to the words in **bold**. You will hear them in the video. Match the words with their definitions below.

‹ Nathan Wolfe is a scientist who studies viruses. A virus is very small. It lives inside other creatures—like bacteria, plants, animals, and people. Some viruses are **deadly**, and can **kill**. Many diseases caused by viruses are difficult to **cure**, but we can **prevent** them from getting into our bodies. In today's globalized[1] world, scientists in different countries can work together more easily to help sick people, but viruses can also **spread** more quickly than ever.

1 When we say the world is **globalized**, we mean technology has made it easy for people to move around and talk to people from other parts of the world.

1. _____: to stop something from happening before it happens
2. _____: very dangerous, able to cause death
3. _____: to increase and happen over a greater area
4. _____: to make a sick person completely well again
5. _____: to cause death

B. Discuss. Nathan Wolfe is the leader of a group of scientists that study viruses. Where do you think these scientists go to study viruses? Discuss your ideas with a partner.

While You Watch

Checking. As you watch the video, check your answers in **Before You Watch B**. Were your ideas correct?

After You Watch

A. Completion. Choose the correct word or phrase to complete each sentence below.

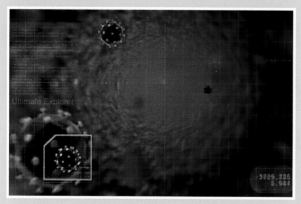

1. Nathan Wolfe and his team study how viruses move from (**animals** / **plants**) into people.

2. According to the video, people who eat (**uncooked food** / **wild animals**) are more likely to get sick from viruses.

3. Wolfe's team believes that many diseases started in a (**warm** / **cold**) place.

4. According to the video, if a deadly virus begins to spread, (**the whole world** / **people living close to animals**) will be in danger.

B. Inferring Meaning. Answer the questions below. Then discuss your answers with a partner.

1. Can viruses be found in chickens?
2. What is one way viruses get from animals into humans?
3. How does a virus spread from country to country?

C. Discuss. Discuss these questions with a partner.

1. What do you think a day in the life of a scientist like Nathan Wolfe is like? Would you like to work with his team?
2. How do you think people can help prevent viruses from spreading?

⌄ A virus can go into a person's blood and make copies of itself.

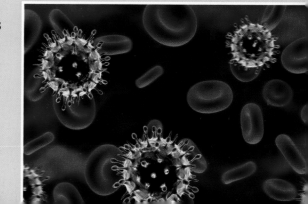

6

EXPLORERS AND PIONEERS

Early European settlers moving across the land in wagons, spread out across North America.

Warm Up

Discuss these questions with a partner.

1. Pioneers are people who explore new places or do things that have never been done before. Do you know about any famous pioneers?

2. Who were the first people to explore, or live in, your country? What stories do you know about them?

Before You Read

A. Matching. Look at the picture and read the caption. Then match the correct form of each word in **bold** with its definition.

1. _____: a piece of metal, usually round, used as money

2. _____: a group of many families with the same language, traditions, and beliefs

3. _____: a piece of art made of stone, metal, or wood, usually showing a person or an animal

B. Skim. Skim the passage on the next page. Check (✓) the information given in the passage. Then read the passage to check your answers.

☐ how Sacagawea helped the explorers

☐ how Sacagawea lived after the trip

☐ how people remember Sacagawea today

∧ In 1804, mapmakers Lewis and Clark began to explore the western part of North America. Sacagawea, a Native American woman from the Shoshone **tribe**, went with them. Today, there are many **statues** of her in the U.S. Her face is also on an American **coin**.

Who was Sacagawea?

1   There are more statues of her than of any other American woman. Her face is on a U.S. coin. **Clearly**, she was an important person. But what do we know about the real Sacagawea?

Sacagawea was part of a Native American tribe called the Shoshone.
5   At the age of 13, she was taken away by people from the Hidatsa tribe. She was living **among** the Hidatsa when Meriwether Lewis and William Clark met her in 1804.

△ The Sacagawea dollar coin was first made in 2000.

Meriwether Lewis and William Clark were mapmakers. These pioneers were exploring the western part of the U.S. Because Sacagawea spoke
10   two different Native American languages, they asked her to **travel** with them, along with her husband and baby son.

Sacagawea became an important part of the group and helped the explorers in many ways. For example, on May 14, 1805, a strong storm tipped over[1] one of their boats. Sacagawea stayed **calm**. She acted
15   quickly and was able to **save** many of the maps and other things from the water. Her **actions** saved important **knowledge** from being lost.

As they traveled, Sacagawea helped Lewis and Clark talk to the Native American people in each **village** they visited. She helped the explorers make friends among the Native Americans, so they could trade with
20   them. She also helped Lewis and Clark find a way across the mountains to the Pacific Ocean, and helped them find food on the way.

∨ Lewis and Clark traveled from St. Louis to the Pacific Ocean and back again.

Sacagawea died when she was about 25. Sadly, we don't know much more about this
25   amazing woman. But two hundred years later, she is remembered as an important woman in U.S. history.

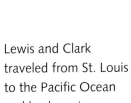

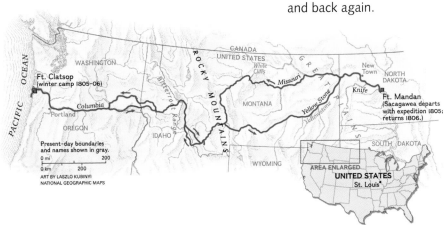

---

1 When something **tips over**, it turns and falls on its side.

Multiple Choice. Choose the best answer for each question.

Gist

1. The reading is mainly about why _____ .
  a. not much is known about Sacagawea
  b. Sacagawea left Lewis and Clark's group
  c. Sacagawea was an important woman in U.S. history

Detail

2. Which of these sentences about Sacagawea is NOT true?
  a. She took her child with her on the trip.
  b. She asked Lewis and Clark if she could come on the trip.
  c. She started living with the Hidatsa tribe when she was 13 years old.

Detail

3. When the explorers' boat tipped over, Sacagawea _____ .
  a. lost all the food they were carrying
  b. was able to save Meriwether Lewis
  c. was able to save maps from the water

Detail

4. Which of the following did Sacagawea do to help Lewis and Clark?
  a. She helped them draw maps of the places they saw.
  b. She helped them make friends with the native people.
  c. She saved their lives when wild animals attacked them.

Vocabulary

5. The word *trade* (line 19) means _____ .
  a. fight
  b. tell stories
  c. buy and sell things

Inference

6. Which of the following sentences is likely to be true?
  a. The author thinks Sacagawea was too young to travel.
  b. The author would like to know more about Sacagawea.
  c. The author believes the story of Sacagawea is not true.

Did You Know?

Lewis kept a journal of the trip. He wrote nearly 5,000 pages.

Creating a Timeline of Events

When you read a passage that has a series of events, it can be useful to place them on a timeline. This gives you a clear picture of what things happened in the order that they happened. Look carefully at ages, dates, and years. But be careful—events may not always appear in the passage in the order that they happened.

A. Scan. Find and underline these events in the reading passage on page 79.

a. The Hidatsa take Sacagawea from her people at age 13.

b. About 200 years ago, Sacagawea dies at about age 25.

c. In 1805, Sacagawea saves maps and other items during a storm.

d. Sacagawea lives among the Shoshone people during her childhood.

e. In 1804, Sacagawea meets Lewis and Clark.

f. With Sacagawea's help, Lewis and Clark reach the Pacific Ocean.

g. Sacagawea joins Lewis and Clark on their trip.

B. Sequencing. Label the timeline with the events in **A**.

☐ ☐ a ☐ ☐ ☐ ☐ ☐

1804

Critical Thinking Discuss with a partner. What do you think Sacagawea's life was like after the expedition? Why do you think we don't know much about Sacagawea's life?

⌃ During the trip, Sacagawea visited her own tribe. Her brother, who was now the chief, was very happy to see her.

Vocabulary Practice

A. Completion. Complete the timeline below with words from the box. Two words are extra.

actions	among	calm	clearly	save	travel	village

Amy Johnson—A Pioneer of Flight

1903   Amy Johnson is born in Hull, England.

1928   She takes flying lessons. She is **1.** _____ not a natural—at first, she is quite bad at it. But she doesn't give up and after a lot of hard work, finally learns to fly.

1930   Johnson becomes the first woman to fly solo[1] from England to Australia. The world starts to take notice of her, and her **2.** _____ inspire many other pilots. When she returns to England, the king and queen are **3.** _____ the many people who send their congratulations.[2]

1931   Johnson is the first person to **4.** _____ from London to Moscow in one day. She then flies across Siberia to Tokyo.

1936   Johnson becomes the first person to fly solo from England to South Africa.

1941   Johnson's plane crashes in the River Thames in London. People from a nearby ship try to **5.** _____ her, but they are too late.

△ Amy Johnson sits aboard her plane.

1 If someone flies **solo**, they fly alone.
2 **Congratulations** are nice messages sent, or things people say, to someone who has done something well.

B. Words in Context. Complete each sentence with the correct word or phrase.

1. Many people think life in a **village** is too _____.
a. quiet   b. noisy

2. If you are **among** friends, you are _____ the group.
a. inside   b. outside

3. If you have great **knowledge** of a subject, you _____.
a. know it well   b. know nothing about it

4. A person _____ is an example of someone who is **calm**.
a. in the middle of a fight   b. who is resting

> **Usage**
> A **town** is usually bigger than a **village**. A **city** is usually bigger than a **town**.
> *About 90 people live in that **village**. Seven thousand people live in my **town**. Tokyo is the world's biggest **city**.*

Polar PIONEER

Before You Read

A. Completion. Read the definitions. Then complete the information below with the correct form of the words in **bold**.

> **on foot:** by walking
>
> **sleds:** objects used for traveling over snow
>
> **team:** a group of people working together
>
> **member:** one of the people that makes up a group

In 1909, Matthew Henson became the first man to reach the North Pole. He did this as a **1.** _____ of a **2.** _____ , led by explorer Robert Peary. To get to the North Pole, the explorers traveled by ship, in **3.** _____ pulled by dogs, and **4.** _____ .

B. Scan. Quickly scan the passage on pages 84–85. In total, how many times did Peary and Henson try to reach the North Pole? Read the passage to check your answer.

In 1937, Matthew Henson was invited to be a member of the Explorers Club. He was the first African American to be invited.

Matthew Henson: Arctic Explorer

1   Robert Peary and Matthew Henson both wanted to be great
explorers. When Peary needed someone to **join** him on his trip to the
North Pole, he thought of Henson. They had once worked together
5   in Central America. At the time, it was unusual for an African
American to be a **well-known** explorer. Henson wanted to change
that. So, though he knew the trip would be hard, he agreed to go.

First, they traveled by ship to Greenland. The members of Peary's
team lived among the Inuit people there. The Inuit called Henson
10   "Maripaluk—Matthew, the Kind One." Henson learned their
language. The Inuit taught him how to live outdoors on the ice, find
food, build igloos,[1] make snowshoes, and **drive** dogsleds through the
snow and ice.

1 An **igloo** is a round
house made of ice.

Robert Peary, the explorer,
stands in Greenland with
his sled dogs.

Among other things,
the explorers' ship, the
Roosevelt, carried over
200 sled dogs.

To the Top of the World

15 Between 1891 and 1906, the Peary-Henson team made seven **attempts** to get to the North Pole. Each time, they learned hard lessons about the dangers there. Sleds broke. Dogs died. Men got hurt. They got close to the North Pole, but they always had to go back.

In 1909, they decided to make one more attempt. Peary and Henson
20 found themselves within 56 kilometers (35 miles) of the North Pole. Peary sent Henson **ahead**. Henson made a **trail** through the snow for Peary to **follow**. Peary followed 45 minutes later. "I think I am the first man to sit on top of the world," Henson told Peary.

The team returned home as **heroes**. Both men's dreams had come true:
25 They were the first explorers to reach the North Pole.

"I think I am the first man to sit on top of the world."

—Matthew Henson,
April 6, 1909

Reading Comprehension

Multiple Choice. Choose the best answer for each question.

Main Idea

1. What is the main idea of the second paragraph (from line 8)?
   a. The Inuit have a difficult life in Greenland.
   b. Henson learned how to speak the Inuit language.
   c. Henson learned many things from the Inuit.

Detail

2. Which of the following sentences about Matthew Henson is true?
   a. He was from Central America.
   b. The Inuit called him "the Kind One."
   c. He was the leader of the team on this trip to the North Pole.

Reference

3. The word *their* in line 10 can be replaced by _____.
   a. the Inuit's
   b. the team's
   c. Peary and Henson's

Vocabulary

4. The phrase *hard lessons* (line 16) refers to _____.
   a. things that are hard to understand
   b. ways they learned to break up hard ice
   c. things they learned because bad things happened

Paraphrase

5. The sentence *Peary sent Henson ahead.* (line 21) is closest in meaning to _____.
   a. Peary sent Henson a message
   b. Peary asked Henson to go first
   c. Peary and Henson traveled together

Inference

6. Which of these statements would Henson likely agree with?
   a. He and Peary were a good team.
   b. Bringing dogs to the North Pole was a bad idea.
   c. The explorers could have reached the North Pole without the help of the Inuit.

Did You Know?

Peary and Henson's 1909 expedition to the North Pole included 19 dogsleds, 133 dogs, and 24 men, including 17 Inuit. Only Peary, Henson, and four Inuit men got to the North Pole.

Understanding Compound Nouns

A compound noun is a word created by putting two words together. It can be formed from different parts of speech, such as a noun + a noun (e.g., *homework*), an adjective + a noun (e.g., *whiteboard*), or a preposition + a noun (e.g., *afternoon*).

A. Noticing. Look back at the second paragraph of the passage on pages 84–85. Find and write the four compound words in the paragraph. Take notice of what smaller words are used to make up each word.

1. _____   3. _____

2. _____   4. _____

B. Completion. Circle the words that create compound nouns. Then write the compound nouns.

1. **class**	(mate)	(room)	student	*classmate*	*classroom*
2. **black**	life	board	bird	_____	_____
3. **out**	side	one	doors	_____	_____
4. **some**	body	day	color	_____	_____
5. **day**	food	time	light	_____	_____
6. **rain**	wet	coat	water	_____	_____
7. **sun**	shine	set	yellow	_____	_____
8. **up**	hill	class	grade	_____	_____

⌄ Matthew Henson sits on his sled, dressed in warm furs.

Critical Thinking Discuss with a partner. Why do you think being an African American explorer in the 1900s was difficult? What qualities do you think Henson had that made him a good explorer?

Vocabulary Practice

A. Matching. Read the information below and match the correct form of each word in **red** with its definition.

Arctic Firsts

Following in the footsteps of Peary and Henson, many people have traveled to the North Pole. Here are some of their stories.

- 60 years after Peary's team, **well-known** British explorer Wally Herbert reached the North Pole. He completed the trip in 1969.

- Teenager Jan Mela became a **hero** to many when he **joined** Polish explorer Marek Kamiński and two others for 2004's "Together to the Pole" trip. They walked to both the North and South Poles in the same year.

- In 2007, a team from the TV show *Top Gear* became the first to **drive** a car to the North Pole. As part of the trip, the team raced against a dogsled. The car won, getting there **ahead** of the sled.

⌃ When he was 13 years old, Jan Mela lost his left leg and right arm. Mela is the youngest person ever to go to both the North and South Poles.

1. _____ : famous

2. _____ : in front of or before something

3. _____ : to become involved in an activity with someone else

4. _____ : someone who does something good, and is admired for it

5. _____ : to operate and control the movement of a car or other vehicle

B. Words in Context. Read the sentences and circle true (**T**) or false (**F**).

1. People usually don't like their **heroes**.   **T**   **F**

2. A **trail** is a route or path, usually for walking.   **T**   **F**

3. If you make an **attempt** to do something, you try to do it.   **T**   **F**

4. When you are **ahead** of someone, they are behind you.   **T**   **F**

5. If you **follow** someone, you walk in front of the person.   **T**   **F**

> **Usage**
>
> You **drive** a car, bus, or truck. You **ride** a bicycle or motorcycle.
>
> *I **drive** a car to work. My brother **rides** a bicycle to school.*

VIEWING Native Americans

Before You Watch

A. Warm Up. Look at the picture and read the caption. What do you know about Native Americans? Discuss with a partner.

< When the first Europeans arrived in North America, they found a population[1] of one million Native Americans already living there. There were many tribes, each with its own culture and language. The new settlers[2] wanted the native peoples' land. There was a lot of fighting between the two groups. The Native American tribes lost their land. Today, many tribes are still trying to win back their land, while others work to rebuild parts of their culture and tribal identity.[3]

---

1 The **population** of a place is the number of people living there.
2 **Settlers** are people who travel to a new place and start to live there.
3 Your **identity** describes who you are.

B. Predict. What do you think happened to the Native Americans after Europeans came to settle in North America? Check (✓) your ideas below.

- [ ] Many of them got sick.
- [ ] They became a single tribe.
- [ ] Many left North America.
- [ ] They taught the settlers about their culture.
- [ ] Their population decreased.
- [ ] They had to leave their homes.
- [ ] They lived in bad conditions.
- [ ] Their culture grew stronger.

While You Watch

Checking. As you watch the video, check your answers in **Before You Watch B**. Were your ideas correct?

After You Watch

A. Sequencing. Read the events described below. Then complete the timeline.

☐   ☐   ☐   ☐   ☐   ☐

1. Humans first come to North America.
2. The first Europeans arrive in North America.
3. Many Native Americans die from new diseases.
4. Traditional art forms and ceremonies begin again.
5. The Native Americans become hundreds of different groups.
6. The government makes the Native Americans leave their land.

B. Completion. Look at the pictures below. Choose the correct word or phrase to complete each sentence.

1. People think the Native Americans came from (**Asia / Europe**).

2. This (**painting / totem pole**) is an example of Native American art.

3. Some tribes have held meetings with (**other tribes / the government**) to talk about getting their land back.

4. The patterns in this picture represent the (**cloud people / Europeans**).

C. Discuss. Discuss these questions with a partner. Who were the first people in your country? Can you still see their culture today?

7

An amazing 3-D drawing on the street plays tricks on our eyes and minds.

MIND'S EYE

Warm Up

Discuss these questions with a partner.

1. What is unusual about the picture above?

2. Do you usually remember your dreams? What is the last dream you remember?

Before You Read

A. Matching. Many people have different ideas about what dreams might mean. Here are some interesting examples. What do you think it might mean if you dream about these things?

1. a snake   •   • a. You're thinking about your mother.

2. a queen   •   • b. You're thinking about a bad memory.

3. your teeth •   • c. You're afraid of something you can't see.

4. a bad smell •   • d. You have trouble sharing your thoughts.

B. Predict. Read the title and headings on the next page, and answer the questions below. Then read the passage to check your ideas.

1. How many kinds of dreams can you read about in the passage?

2. What do you think the passage will tell you about each type of dream?

The Meaning of Dreams

1 Did you have any interesting dreams last night?

Our dreams come from a part of the brain that contains our thoughts and memories. A person can have up to six dreams a night, and each dream usually **lasts** from 10 to 40 minutes. Everyone dreams, but not

5 everyone remembers their dreams. Most people dream in color, usually with sound. And we usually dream about ourselves and the people we know.

Why Do We Dream?

Alan Siegel is a scientist who studies dreams. "Dreams help us get

10 in touch with our deeper feelings," he says. "They can tell us a lot about ourselves, and can help us figure out **problems**." Another scientist, Robert Stickgold, thinks dreams come from our memories. He believes we dream to remember, because memories are **useful** to the brain. Stickgold says the purpose of dreaming through these

15 memories is to help us learn from the past.

Here are a few types of dreams and what people think they mean.

Dream 1: You Meet Someone While in Your Pajamas[1]

Sometimes people dream that they meet someone they know while wearing their underwear (or nothing at all!). This dream may be the

20 **result** of an embarrassing[2] event in your life. Some people think we dream about embarrassing situations if our brains are trying to deal with[3] an event in our own lives.

Dream 2: You're Flying

If you dream about flying, you are probably quite happy. This is a

25 good **period** in your life. You may feel that other people see you as a **leader**.

Dream 3: You Didn't Study for a Test

This probably means you are **worried** about an important event coming in your life. If you're not **prepared** for the event, your dream

30 may be telling you, "It's time to get to work!"

---

1 **Pajamas** are clothes that are specially made to sleep in.

2 If something is **embarrassing**, it makes you feel shy or ashamed.

3 If you **deal with** a problem, you try to do something about it.

Reading Comprehension

Multiple Choice. Choose the best answer for each question.

Main Idea   **1.** What is the main idea of the reading?
- a. Dreams come from only one part of the brain.
- b. Everyone has dreams, but not everyone remembers them.
- c. Dreams can help us to understand our feelings and problems.

Detail   **2.** Which of these sentences about dreams is NOT true?
- a. They usually have color and sound.
- b. Each dream usually lasts for 10 to 40 minutes.
- c. Most people have about ten dreams a night.

Detail   **3.** Robert Stickgold believes that dreams _____ .
- a. can tell us about ourselves
- b. help us figure out problems
- c. are made from our memories

Vocabulary   **4.** In lines 9–10, another way to say *get in touch with* would be _____ .
- a. talk to
- b. dream about
- c. find out and understand

Detail   **5.** According to the passage, which of these sentences is true?
- a. If you dream you're wearing no clothes, something embarrassing probably happened to you.
- b. If you dream you're flying, this is probably a difficult time in your life.
- c. If you dream you didn't study for a test, you're probably not getting enough sleep at night.

Inference   **6.** If someone says, "The concert is tomorrow, and I haven't had time to practice!" which dream from the passage might they have?
- a. Dream 1: You Meet Someone While in Your Pajamas
- b. Dream 2: You're Flying
- c. Dream 3: You Didn't Study for a Test

Did You Know?

Most people forget half of their dreams within five minutes of waking up. After ten minutes, 90 percent of their dreams are usually gone.

Creating a Concept Map

A concept map helps you organize information in a visual way. To create a concept map, start by writing the general topic or main idea of the text in a center box. Then write other key ideas related to this around the box, linking with lines to show relationships. After that, add and link additional details. Generally, ideas in a concept map move from general to specific as you move outward from the center.

Scientists have found that animals have dreams, too. While they sleep, their brain waves show that they're dreaming, and that the part of the brain that stores memories is being used. This suggests they dream about things that happened while they were awake.

A. Analyzing. Look back at the reading passage on page 93. What information is important to remember? Circle the main ideas and underline the key details.

B. Completion. Complete the concept map with words from the reading passage.

can have six dreams a night, each lasts up to **1.** _____

to get in touch with feelings

everyone dreams, but not all **2.** _____ their dreams

Facts about dreams

3. _____ **we dream**

to figure out **4.** _____

we dream about ourselves and people we know

Dreams

to remember

5. The _____ **of dreams**

meet someone while in pajamas = probably the result of a(n) **6.** _____ situation

flying = probably feel quite **7.** _____ ; a good time in your life

didn't study for test = probably **8.** _____ about an important event

Critical Thinking Discuss with a partner. Which idea from the passage on page 93—Stickgold's or Siegel's—do you believe? Do you think dreams have meaning?

Vocabulary Practice

A. Definitions. Use the correct form of the words in the box to complete the definitions below.

> last   leader   period   prepare   problem   result   useful   worried

1. A _____ is something caused by something else.

2. If a class _____ one hour, it's 60 minutes long.

3. If something is _____ , it's helpful in some way.

4. If you _____ for something, you get ready for it.

5. Someone who fears something bad will happen is probably _____ .

6. _____ are things that are difficult to deal with.

7. A _____ of time is a length of time in which something happens.

8. A _____ is someone who others follow.

B. Completion. Complete the information below with the correct form of the words from the box in **A**.

We spend about one-third of our lives sleeping. Children usually need a lot of sleep because they are still growing. Older people need to sleep for shorter **1.** _____ of time. In general, sleep that **2.** _____ seven or eight hours is enough for most people.

However, a lot of people don't get enough sleep. This causes **3.** _____ for the part of the brain that controls our emotions. For example, one of the **4.** _____ of not getting enough sleep is that we can become angry or **5.** _____ more easily.

If you have trouble sleeping, you can **6.** _____ for sleep by taking a warm bath or listening to slow music. Some people find it **7.** _____ to drink warm milk.

∧ A glass of warm milk helps some people fall asleep. Milk contains melatonin, a chemical that causes us to feel sleepy.

> **Word Partnership**
> Use **problem** with: (*v.*) **cause** a problem, **solve** a problem, **fix** a problem; (*adj.*) **big** problem, **serious** problem, **major** problem, **common** problem.

Seeing the IMPOSSIBLE

Before You Read

A. Discussion. Look at the picture above and read the caption. Then answer the questions below.

1. Can you explain what you see? How do you think this photo was taken?

2. Have you seen photos with illusions like this before?

B. Predict. Look at the title and the pictures on pages 97–99. What is unusual about each picture? Discuss each picture with a partner. Then read the passage to check your ideas.

∧ This photo was taken in the middle of Salar de Uyuni, the world's largest salt flat, in Bolivia. In the dry season, the area is completely flat and white, making photos like this one possible.

1　Can you believe everything you see? Not always! Sometimes our minds and our eyes make **mistakes**. At other times, our eyes and minds can become confused.[1] This may be because we are looking at something called an *optical illusion*.

5　The word *optical* means "**related to** sight"—the way we see things with our eyes. An *illusion* is something that looks different from the way it really is. In short, an optical illusion is a kind of trick that our eyes play on us.

Look at these optical illusions and compare what you see with what
10　your classmates see. The way we see things is often **personal**, so you may not see things the same way as someone else.

So can you **trust** your eyes? Perhaps the answer is "sometimes." Sometimes our eyes see something, and our minds understand it easily. At other times, we may need to look twice.

1 If you **confuse** two things, you get them mixed up.

15 ┃ Which red dot is larger?

Most people say it's the dot on the left. Now measure the dots. The red dot on the left may seem larger because of the small blue dots around it, but they're really the
20　same **size**.

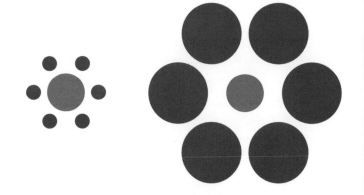

┃ Look at this picture. What do you see?

Do you see a cup, or do you see two faces? Now look again! The illusion shows
25　two different images at the same time. **Therefore**, our minds have to choose which image to look at. Scientists think this choice is difficult, because different parts of your brain are getting different information.
30　One part "sees" the cup and another part "sees" the faces, so the image keeps changing.

Are the circles moving?

When you **stare** at this picture, your mind may tell you that the
35   circles are moving, but this is **impossible**! How can a picture move?
Some people think the circles seem to move because, often, when
we see circle-in-circle shapes, like in car wheels or snake bodies, they
are usually moving. Our brains are used to seeing these shapes move.
So when our eyes see this shape, our mind infers that the image is
40   moving. Other scientists believe the illusion of movement is caused
by the tiny movements of our eyes as we look at the different colors
and patterns of the picture.

Reading Comprehension

Multiple Choice. Choose the best answer for each question.

Main Idea | **1.** What is the main idea of the first paragraph?
- a. Optical illusions can only be seen by a few people.
- b. Optical illusions are things that aren't real.
- c. Optical illusions make us think we see something that's not there.

Detail | **2.** What causes optical illusion 1 (from line 15)?
- a. The red dots aren't close to each other.
- b. We can see the blue dots clearly, but not the red dots.
- c. We compare each red dot with the blue dots around it.

Reference | **3.** The word *they're* (line 19) refers to the _____ .
- a. red dots
- b. big blue dots
- c. small blue dots

Detail | **4.** What causes optical illusion 2 (from line 21)?
- a. Your left and right eyes see different things.
- b. Different parts of your brain get different information.
- c. Your brain thinks that it can see faces that aren't really there.

Vocabulary | **5.** In line 41, the word *tiny* can be replaced with _____ .
- a. very fast
- b. very small
- c. very strange

Inference | **6.** Which of these is an optical illusion?
- a. hearing a voice in your head that isn't there
- b. seeing water on a road when it's not really there
- c. looking up at a strange cloud and noticing its shape

Did You Know?

3-D movies are a type of optical illusion.

Understanding Compound Sentences

A compound sentence consists of two simple sentences joined by a comma and a conjunction. Conjunctions include *and* (to add information), *but* (to contrast information), *or* (to show a choice), and *so* (to show a result). Look at these examples.

I want to buy a new dictionary, **and** *I need some new notebooks.*
I want to buy a new dictionary, **but** *I don't have any money.*
I might just buy a new dictionary, **or** *I might just borrow my friend's.*
I want to buy a new dictionary, **so** *I'm going to go to the bookstore.*

⌃ This fountain in Ypres, Belgium, forms an optical illusion, that of a floating faucet.

A. Completion. Circle the correct conjunction to complete each sentence.

1. I like optical illusions. They're interesting to look at, (**and / or**) they can be a lot of fun.

2. You can find optical illusions in books, (**or / so**) you can look for them online.

3. Optical illusions play tricks on the mind, (**but / so**) they can make people very confused.

4. Optical illusions use color, light, and patterns, (**and / but**) they don't use sound.

B. Completion. Complete these sentences using words from the box. Then look back at the reading on pages 98–99 to check your answers.

> or   so   but   and

1. Sometimes our eyes see something, _____ our minds understand it easily. (lines 13–14)

2. The red dot on the left may seem larger because of the small blue dots around it, _____ they're really the same size. (lines 17–20)

3. Do you see a cup, _____ do you see two faces? (lines 23–24)

4. One part "sees" the cup and another part "sees" the faces, _____ the image keeps changing. (line 30–32)

Critical Thinking Discuss with a partner. Look back at the optical illusions on pages 98–99. Which of the illusions is most confusing to you? Why?

Vocabulary Practice

A. Completion. Choose the correct words to complete the information below.

Look at the photo. What do you see? Do you **1.** (**trust** / **stare**) your eyes? Maybe you shouldn't. Your eyes—and your mind—might be making a **2.** (**stare** / **mistake**).

If you see only dark camels crossing the desert, your eyes are playing tricks on you. The photographer took this photo toward the end of the day. **3.** (**Impossible** / **Therefore**), the sun was low in the sky and the camels had long shadows. The dark camel shapes you see in the photo are really just the camels' shadows. If you **4.** (**trust** / **stare**) at it closely, you can see that the real camels are the thin brown shapes below the darker camel shapes.

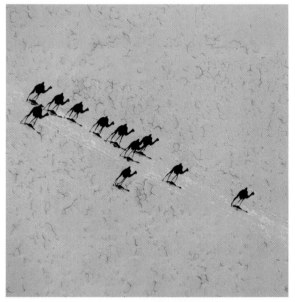

⌃ This photo of camels walking in the desert forms a kind of optical illusion. Sometimes optical illusions happen naturally.

B. Words in Context. Complete each sentence with the correct answer.

1. An idea that is **related to** something is _____ that thing.
   a. linked with   b. different from

2. It is **impossible** for an elephant to _____.
   a. carry a tree branch   b. carry a large whale

3. The **size** of something is how _____ it is.
   a. heavy   b. big

4. When you **stare** at something, you look at it for a _____ time.
   a. short   b. long

5. If you make a **mistake**, you do something that is _____.
   a. correct   b. wrong

6. If something is **personal**, you _____.
   a. share it with everyone   b. keep it to yourself

> **Word Partnership**
> Use *mistake* with: (*v.*) **make** a mistake, **correct** a mistake, **repeat** a mistake; (*adj.*) **terrible** mistake, **stupid** mistake, **common** mistake.

VIEWING Parasomnia

Before You Watch

A. Warm Up. Look at the picture and read the caption. Have you, or anyone you know, experienced parasomnia? Discuss with a partner.

< Have you ever seen someone walking around while they're asleep? Their eyes may be open, but they don't seem to see anything. It may sound strange, but many people do get out of bed and move around without ever waking up. Sleepwalking is an example of a type of sleep problem called *parasomnia*. Other people who have parasomnia may move around in their sleep and seem to be having nightmares (bad dreams), or move their legs as if they are kicking something.

B. Predict. Answer the questions below. Discuss with a partner.

1. What causes people to experience parasomnia?
   a. They have slept for too long.
   b. A part of their brain is awake.
   c. They're having a very scary dream.

2. Which of these is another example of parasomnia?
   a. snoring very loudly
   b. eating while sleeping
   c. waking up many times in one night

While You Watch

A. Checking. As you watch the video, check your answers in **Before You Watch B**. Were your ideas correct?

B. Viewing. What other kinds of sleep activities does the video mention?
   ☐ fighting   ☐ cooking   ☐ dancing   ☐ talking   ☐ driving

After You Watch

A. Multiple Choice. Choose the correct answer for each question below.

1. The video says people who fight in their sleep may _____ .

   a. be angry with their partner

   b. be worried about a problem

   c. be dreaming about being attacked

2. When people with parasomnia wake up they _____ .

   a. think they're still in a dream

   b. remember their dreams clearly

   c. don't know what they have done

3. When people sleepwalk, their _____ is awake.

   a. upper brain   b. middle brain   c. lower brain

B. Matching. Match the stages of NREM sleep with their descriptions.

Stage 1	Stage 2	Stages 3 and 4

1. Your body relaxes.

2. You're in deep sleep.

3. You sleep lightly.

4. Brain waves are small.

5. Heart beat and breathing get slower.

6. Brain waves are large and far apart.

7. Your brain shuts off sounds and movements from the outside world.

C. Discuss. Discuss these questions with a partner.

1. What do you think you should do if you see someone with parasomnia?

2. The video says parasomnia can be dangerous. In what ways do you think parasomnia can be dangerous?

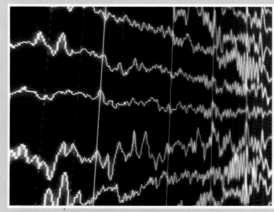

⋀ This pattern of lines shows a person's brain waves as he or she goes from R.E.M. sleep to waking up.

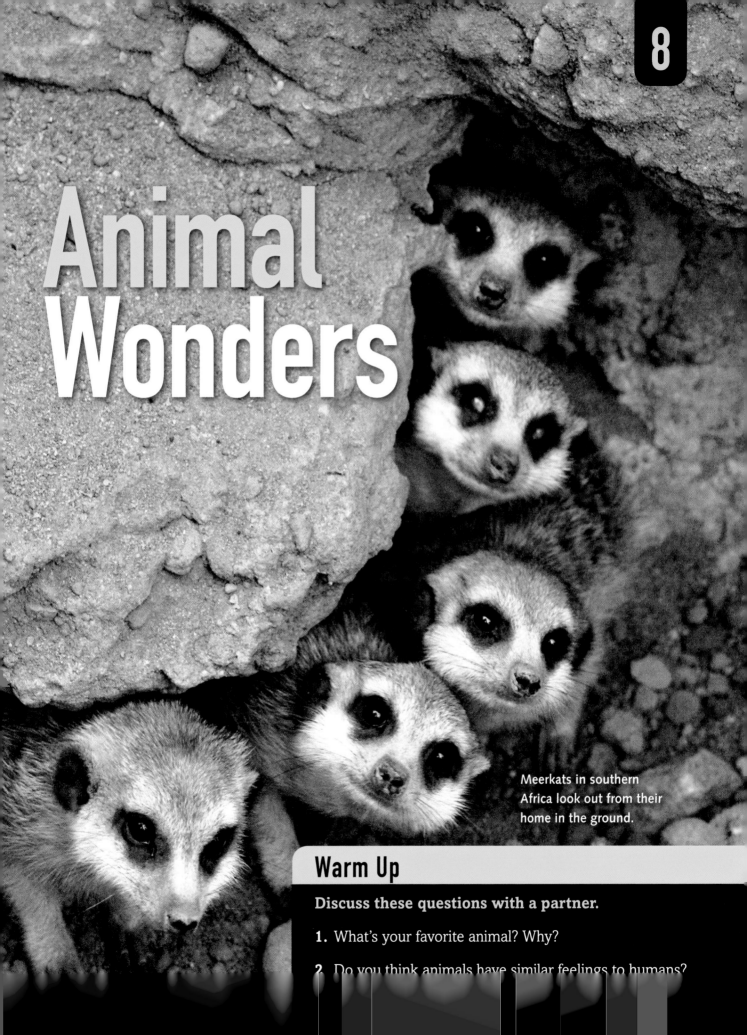

8

Animal Wonders

Meerkats in southern Africa look out from their home in the ground.

Warm Up

Discuss these questions with a partner.

1. What's your favorite animal? Why?

2. Do you think animals have similar feelings to humans?

In Antarctica, home of the emperor penguin, it can get as cold as -60°C (-75°F).

Before You Read

A. Quiz. What do you know about penguins?
Mark each sentence below as true (**T**) or false (**F**).

1. Penguins can breathe underwater.   **T**   **F**
2. Wild penguins only live in Antarctica.   **T**   **F**
3. There are six different types of penguins.   **T**   **F**
4. Once a year, penguins lose all their feathers.   **T**   **F**
5. Penguins feed their babies food that they already ate.   **T**   **F**

B. Predict. Look quickly at the photos and headings on pages 107–108. Check (✓) the information you think you'll read about. Then read the passage to check your answers.

☐   emperor penguins and their babies

☐   young penguins getting older

☐   global warming and penguins

A Penguin Family

1   Emperor penguins are the largest penguins on Earth. Each
adult is over a meter tall, and can weigh[1] up to 40 kilograms.

Antarctica

For many months each year, emperors live near the sea in
large groups called *colonies*. However, in May, the weather
5   gets colder and ice covers large areas of ocean. Each colony
moves many kilometers from the water. There, each mother
penguin lays[2] just one egg. Then all the hungry mothers must
walk back to the ocean to find food. The father penguins put
their eggs on top of their feet, under a **special** piece of skin
10   called the *brood pouch*.

Sharing the Work

For two months, the father penguins keep the eggs safe and
warm. They do this through some of the coldest weather
conditions on Earth. By July, it is winter in Antarctica. Most
15   animals leave for warmer places, but the father penguins stay.
In this time, without food, a father penguin can lose almost
half of his body weight.

1 If something **weighs** 40
kilograms, that is how
heavy it is.

2 When an animal **lays an
egg**, it pushes it out from
its body.

New Life

By August, the babies begin to hatch![3] The mother penguin returns just in time to see her baby come out of its egg. The chick[4] is then moved to her brood pouch. This can be difficult. If the chick falls, it can freeze[5] quickly, so the penguin **parents** must be very **careful**. Once this is done, the father penguin can go back to the ocean to find food.

Growing Up

Over the next few months, penguin parents **take turns** going to the ocean for food. They each make the trip **several** times, bringing back food for the chick. The chick grows quickly and is always hungry.

Into the Water

By December, winter is ending. The chick is five months old and can live **on its own**. Soon it **enters** the water for the first time. It will swim and eat until next April, and then return here. After a few more years, it, too, will start its own family.

---

3 If baby animals **hatch**, they come out of an egg.
4 A **chick** is a baby bird.
5 If a liquid **freezes**, it becomes solid like ice because of low temperatures.

A family of emperor penguins—mother, father, and baby—stands close together to keep warm.

Reading Comprehension

Multiple Choice. Choose the best answer for each question.

Gist

1. Another good title for this passage would be _____ .
   a. A Study of Penguin Families
   b. Types of Penguins Around the World
   c. Emperor Penguins and Global Warming

Sequence

2. Which of the following things happens first?
   a. The adult penguins walk away from the ocean.
   b. The mother penguin walks to the ocean to find food.
   c. The father penguin loses half of his body weight.

Detail

3. When does the father penguin care for the egg without the mother penguin?
   a. from May to August
   b. from August to October
   c. from October to December

Vocabulary

4. The word *almost* (line 16) means _____ .
   a. nearly
   b. exactly
   c. more than

Inference

5. What will probably happen if the chick falls onto the ice?
   a. Another penguin will take the chick.
   b. The chick will die because of the cold.
   c. The father penguin cannot go find food.

Reference

6. The word *here* (line 31) refers to _____ .
   a. the water
   b. where it grew up
   c. where it learned to swim

Did You Know?

As young penguins grow, the adults leave them in groups of chicks called *crèches*. Some adults stay behind to care for the chicks.

Reading Skill

Paraphrasing

A paraphrased sentence has the same meaning as the original sentence, but uses different words and (sometimes) different grammar. Paraphrasing can make a passage more interesting. Look at this example.

Original: Emperor penguins are the largest penguins on Earth.

Paraphrased: There are no penguins on Earth larger than emperor penguins.

A. Multiple Choice. Which sentence correctly paraphrases the first? Circle **a** or **b**.

1. Penguins cannot fly.
   a. Penguins are not able to fly.
   b. Penguins swim but don't fly.

2. Penguins get all their food from the sea.
   a. Penguins get some food on land.
   b. Penguins only find food in the sea.

3. Penguins prefer to be around other penguins.
   a. Penguins are never alone.
   b. Penguins like to be in groups.

B. Completion. Look back at the passage on pages 107–108. Find and underline sentences from the passage that match what these paraphrased sentences mean.

1. The father penguin takes care of the egg for two months.
2. The mother penguin comes back from the ocean before the egg hatches.
3. It's not easy to do this.
4. The baby is getting bigger fast and needs a lot of food.
5. The baby is older and is living without its parents.

Critical Thinking Discuss with a partner. Which do you think is the more important penguin parent—the mother or the father? Why?

Vocabulary Practice

A. Matching. Read the information below and match each word in **red** with its definition.

- Siberian tigers are the largest tigers in the world. An **adult** male's body can grow to three meters (ten feet).
- Each tiger has a **special** pattern of black and orange marks on its fur. These make them difficult to see among the trees.
- Tigers generally like to live **on their own**. They leave their **parents** when they are still young.
- Most other cats do not like to **enter** water, but tigers love to swim.
- There are about 500 Siberian tigers in Asia, but few live in the wild. Most live in zoos today.

1. _____: father and mother

2. _____: not a child; fully grown

3. _____: alone, not with anyone else

4. _____: unusual; not like other kinds

5. _____: to go into (something)

B. Words in Context. Complete each sentence with the correct answer.

1. If you have **several** pets, you have _____ pets.
   a. one or two   b. more than two

2. If you and a friend **take turns** riding a bike, you ride it _____ .
   a. one after the other   b. at the same time

3. You need to be **careful** when you are _____ .
   a. carrying a glass statue b. trying to fall asleep

4. When you **enter** someone's house, you go _____ .
   a. outside   b. inside

> **Word Partnership**
> Use **enter** with: (*n.*) enter a **room**, enter **school**, enter **college**, enter a **contest**.

∧ Today, wild Siberian tigers are found only in an area called Primorsky Krai, in Russia. It is very cold there, but the tigers' thick fur keeps them warm.

⌃ Through their faces and body language, animals often seem to show very humanlike emotions.

Before You Read

A. Discussion. Look at the photos above. Which word(s) in the box could describe each animal? Do you think animals really have these feelings?

> anger boredom happiness surprise

B. Scan. Quickly scan the passage on the next page. Underline the names you find. How many are there? Which are pets, and which are humans? Read the passage to check your answers.

Do Animals LAUGH?

1 We know animals have **emotions**. They can feel fear. We also think they feel love, since they have strong **relationships** with each other. So are animal emotions all **similar** to our own? And do animals have a sense of humor?[1]

A Parrot Named Bongo Marie

Sally Blanchard's parrot Bongo Marie didn't **get along** with her other parrot, Paco. In fact, Bongo Marie clearly didn't like Paco at all! One day, Blanchard cooked a chicken for dinner. She started to cut the chicken with a knife. "Oh, no! Paco!"
10 Bongo Marie said loudly and **laughed**. Blanchard laughed, too, and said, "That's not Paco." "Oh . . . no," said Bongo Marie. This time, she sounded disappointed.[2] Then the parrot laughed at her own joke.[3]

Yoga Dog

15 Jean Donaldson enjoys doing yoga—and so does her dog Buffy. While Jean Donaldson does yoga, Buffy carefully places her **toys** on Donaldson's body. If a toy falls, Buffy runs to put it back. Does this **behavior** have any real purpose? "She thinks it's hilarious!"[4] says Donaldson.

Animal Laughter

Can dogs "laugh"? Recent research shows that dogs can tell each other when they want to play. They make a special sound—a kind of "laugh." Psychologist Patricia Simonet recorded the sound. Then she played it back to dogs to
25 **assess** their behavior. "All the dogs seemed to like the laugh," says Simonet. So do animals have a sense of humor? If laughter is a clue, then perhaps the answer is "yes!"

Do dogs really laugh?

1 Someone's **sense of humor** is their ability to know what is funny.

2 If someone is **disappointed**, they are sad they didn't get what they wanted.

3 A **joke** is something that makes you laugh.

4 If something is **hilarious**, it is very funny.

Reading Comprehension

Multiple Choice. Choose the best answer for each question.

Gist

1. What does the author want to know?
   a. Do animals have emotions?
   b. Do animals have a sense of humor?
   c. Do animals laugh in the same way as humans?

Detail

2. Which of the following sentences is NOT true?
   a. Paco and Bongo Marie are both parrots.
   b. Paco and Bongo Marie are good friends.
   c. Sally Blanchard thinks Bongo Marie is funny.

Reference

3. The word *she* (line 12) refers to _____ .
   a. Paco
   b. Bongo Marie
   c. Sally Blanchard

Detail

4. Which of the following sentences is true?
   a. Buffy feels sad when Jean Donaldson does yoga.
   b. Jean Donaldson thinks Buffy has a sense of humor.
   c. Buffy laughs at Jean Donaldson when she does yoga.

Vocabulary

5. In line 24, the phrase *played it back* is closest in meaning to _____ .
   a. recorded it again
   b. played with the dogs
   c. let the dogs hear the recording

Main Idea

6. What is the main idea of the last paragraph?
   a. A scientist showed that dogs talk to each other, so they seem to be funnier than most animals.
   b. A scientist showed that dogs make a laughing sound, so animals might really have a sense of humor.
   c. A scientist recorded dogs making a laughing sound, but doesn't believe they have a sense of humor.

Did You Know?

Most African Grey Parrots, like Bongo Marie, are able to learn a few words, but some have a vocabulary of over 500 words and phrases.

Reading Skill

Identifying Supporting Details

It's important to identify the main idea of a passage. But it's also important to identify details that support that idea. These might include reasons, examples, facts, or descriptions. As you read, ask yourself how well the author supports the main idea of the passage.

A. Analyzing. Circle the letters of the statements that support the idea "Elephants are very smart animals."

a. Elephants can live for 60 to 80 years in the wild.

b. Elephants know themselves when they look in a mirror.

c. Elephants can paint pictures and play music.

d. Elephants pull off tree branches and use them to keep flies away.

e. Elephants live in both Africa and Asia.

f. Elephants usually have a good sense of humor.

g. People often kill elephants for their tusks.

B. Completion. In the passage on page 113, the author asks, "Do animals have a sense of humor?" Complete the information below with words from the passage.

∧ A picture of some flowers painted by an elephant

Sally Blanchard owns two parrots named Bongo Marie and Paco. One day, Bongo Marie told a **1.** _____ and then she **2.** _____ .

Jean Donaldson's dog Buffy likes to put **3.** _____ on Jean's body while she does yoga. If one falls, Buffy puts it back. Jean says that Buffy thinks this is **4.** _____ .

Psychologist Patricia Simonet thinks that dogs make a sound that is similar to a human **5.** _____ . The sound lets other dogs know when they want to **6.** _____ .

Critical Thinking Discuss with a partner. Do you think the supporting details in **B** helped you answer the question, "Do animals have a sense of humor?" Have you ever seen animals show emotions? Describe the situations.

Vocabulary Practice

A. Completion. Complete the sentences with the correct words from the box. One word is extra.

assess	behavior	laughter	relationship	similar

Chimpanzees are **1.** _____ to humans in many ways. For example, the **2.** _____ between chimps is often very close. This was clear when researchers studied a pair of brother and sister chimps, Kanzi and Panbanisha.

The researchers wanted to **3.** _____ how well the chimps had learned to make stone knives. So they gave each chimp a box with a banana in it. They also gave the chimps the items they needed to make knives, to cut open the boxes.

Kanzi made a good knife, but his sister could not. When he saw that she was sad, Kanzi tried to give his knife to her. When no one was looking, he put his knife where his sister could find it, and she finally got her banana. Kanzi's **4.** _____ showed the researchers that he cared for his sister.

∧ Kanzi the bonobo can make knives from stone, play music, and understand more than 500 English words.

B. Words in Context. Read the sentences below. Then mark each sentence as true (**T**) or false (**F**).

1. If you **get along** with someone, you often fight with them. **T** **F**
2. If you **assess** something, you test or measure it. **T** **F**
3. A **toy** is something you can play with. **T** **F**
4. Two things that are **similar** are the same in some way. **T** **F**
5. **Emotions** are different from thoughts. **T** **F**
6. The sound of **laughter** is usually a happy sound. **T** **F**

> **Word Partnership**
> Use **similar** with: **be + similar + to**, e.g., *Animals are **similar** to humans in some ways.*

VIEWING Penguins in Trouble

Before You Watch

A. Warm Up. Look at the picture and read the caption. How do you think a leopard seal catches a penguin? Discuss with a partner.

∧ Because their food comes from the sea, penguins spend as much as half their lives swimming. In the water, penguins can reach speeds of up to 27 kilometers per hour (17 miles per hour). However, this speed can't always save them from predators like the leopard seal. Leopard seals may seem too big to move quickly, but they can often move quickly enough to catch penguins. And penguins are one of their favorite meals.

B. Quiz. What do you know about leopard seals? Answer the questions below. Then check your answers at the bottom of page 118.

1. Adult (**female / male**) leopard seals are larger.
2. Leopard seals usually live (**on their own / in groups**).
3. A baby leopard seal is called a (**cub / pup**).
4. Leopard seals eat penguins, birds, and (**small whales / other seals**).

While You Watch

True or False. As you watch the video, mark each sentence below as true (**T**) or false (**F**).

In the video . . .

1. There is only one leopard seal but many penguins. **T** **F**
2. The penguins jump onto land, but the seal does not. **T** **F**
3. The seal catches two penguins. **T** **F**
4. The seal goes away hungry. **T** **F**

After You Watch

A. Cause and Effect. Match the causes with their effects.

Causes	so	Effects
1. the baby penguins are hungry	• •	a. they turn around fast
2. a leopard seal waits nearby	• •	b. they cannot move very fast
3. more penguins arrive, but they sense the leopard seal	• •	c. the penguins are in danger
4. the penguin that is caught relaxes its body	• •	d. the penguin parents have to fish
5. the penguins and seal are out of their usual environment, the water	• •	e. it can escape when the seal drops it

B. Paraphrasing. Use the information above to help you describe the events of the video in your own words to a partner.

C. Discuss. Discuss these questions with a partner.

1. The video says, "In Antarctica, every day is a fight for survival." What do you think this means?

2. How did you feel when the leopard seal caught the penguin or when the penguin got away? Why?

A leopard seal swims away with its lunch. ❯

1. female; 2. on their own; 3. pup; 4. other seals

9

INCREDIBLE DOMES

High above Red Square in Moscow, Russia, the great domes of Saint Basil's Cathedral stand as reminders of Russia's colorful past.

Warm Up

Discuss these questions with a partner.

1. What do you think is the most interesting thing about this building?

2. What is the most famous building in your country? Why?

Before You Read

A. Matching. Look at the picture and read the information below. Match the words in **bold** with their definitions.

The Taj Mahal in Agra, India, is one of the most famous **monuments** in the world. The **emperor** Shah Jahan built the Taj Mahal from white **marble**. The large **dome** at its center is one of the most famous parts of the building.

1. _____ : the male ruler of an empire

2. _____ : a rounded roof

3. _____ : a type of stone often used in buildings

4. _____ : large structures built to remind people of a famous event or person

B. Predict. Look at the title, photos, and captions on this page and the next. Why do you think Shah Jahan built the Taj Mahal? Read the passage to check your ideas.

The Taj Mahal was built by the emperor Shah Jahan for the love of his life, Arjumand Banu Begum. The empress is more famously known as Mumtaz Mahal—*Chosen One of the Palace.*

A Love Poem in Stone

1　Often called "a love poem[1] in stone," the Taj Mahal is well-known for being one of the most beautiful buildings ever created. It is also perhaps the most beautiful **expression** of love in the world.

A painted picture of Shah Jahan and Mumtaz Mahal

5　The emperor Shah Jahan built the Taj Mahal for his empress, Mumtaz Mahal. The **couple** lived happily together for 18 years. Then Mumtaz died during the **birth** of their fourteenth child. Before she died, the emperor made her a **promise**. To remember her,
10　he would build the most beautiful monument in the world.

The emperor poured his passion and wealth into building the Taj Mahal. It is said that it took more than 20,000 people and 1,000 elephants to build. They worked for over 20 years to build the monument and its
15　central dome, which stands over 73 meters above the ground.

Soon after the building was **finished**, Shah Jahan's son became emperor. He put Shah Jahan in prison.[2] Shah Jahan lived there until his death in 1666, when his body was put in the Taj Mahal with the woman he loved.

20　There are many **legends** about the Taj Mahal. In one story, when the building was complete, Shah Jahan had the builders' hands cut off, **supposedly** so they could never build anything as beautiful as the Taj Mahal. Another says he also wanted to build a black Taj Mahal. These are interesting stories, but they are most likely not true.

25　The love story between Shah Jahan and his wife ended sadly. But the monument to their love still stands today. It is visited by millions of **tourists**, who come to see the marble change color in the light of the rising sun or a full moon.

1　A **poem** is a piece of writing that usually has rhythm; something beautiful.

2　A **prison** is a place where people who break the law are kept, where they cannot get out.

Reading Comprehension

Multiple Choice. Choose the best answer for each question.

Gist

1. What could be another title for this reading?
   a. The Emperor and Empress's Home
   b. How an Emperor Showed His Love
   c. The Beautiful Writings of Shah Jahan

Sequence

2. When was the Taj Mahal built?
   a. after the death of Mumtaz Mahal
   b. when Shah Jahan's son became emperor
   c. while Shah Jahan was in prison

Paraphrase

3. What is another way of saying *It is said that* (line 13)?
   a. It is true that
   b. We said that
   c. Some people believe that

Reference

4. Who does the word *He* refer to in line 17?
   a. Shah Jahan
   b. Shah Jahan's son
   c. Shah Jahan's father

Detail

5. Which of these statements about the Taj Mahal is true?
   a. It took 20 years to build.
   b. Shah Jahan died inside it in 1666.
   c. Its central dome was never completed.

Main Idea

6. What is the main idea of the fifth paragraph (from line 20)?
   a. The Taj Mahal has a very dark and sad history.
   b. Shah Jahan was known to be a terrible person.
   c. There are many stories about the Taj Mahal, many untrue.

Did You Know?

Shah Jahan used 28 different kinds of gems and stones to make the inside of the Taj Mahal beautiful. These gems and stones came from many places, including China, Afghanistan, Sri Lanka, and Arabia.

Understanding Complex Sentences

Compound sentences consist of two independent clauses (see Unit 7). *Complex* sentences, on the other hand, consist of an **independent clause** and a **dependent clause** connected by a **conjunction**. Conjunctions include *before, after, when, while* (to show time), *if* (to show condition), *because* (to show a reason), and *but* or *although* (to show a contrast). In these examples, the dependent clause is underlined.

I plan to go on a trip <u>after I save enough money</u>.
<u>If I save enough</u>, I want to visit Florence.
I want to go there <u>because I'm very interested in art</u>.
<u>Although I speak Italian</u>, I'm going to take a phrase book with me.

A. Scan. Look back at the passage on page 121. Complete each sentence with a conjunction.

1. _____ Mumtaz Mahal died, the emperor made her a promise. (lines 8–9)

2. _____ the Taj Mahal was finished, Shah Jahan's son became emperor. (lines 16–17)

3. In one story, _____ the building was complete, Shah Jahan had the builders' hands cut off. (lines 20–21)

4. There are many interesting stories about the Taj Mahal, _____ they are most likely not true. (lines 23–24)

B. Completion. Choose the correct conjunctions to complete the information.

Tips for Visiting the Taj Mahal

1. Enter through the south gates (**because / although**) there are usually long lines at the east and west gates.

2. (**When / Because**) you visit, keep the areas inside and outside clean.

3. Take off your shoes (**although / before**) you enter.

4. You can also wear shoe covers (**while / before**) you are inside.

5. Do not bring video cameras (**while / because**) they are not allowed inside.

6. (**If / Although**) it is not required, consider hiring a guide.

7. (**Before / If**) you hire a guide, hire only the ones with official I.D. cards.

8. Do not touch the walls (**when / because**) this can harm the monument.

Critical Thinking Discuss with a partner. Do you know of any other famous or interesting ways that people have expressed their love?

Vocabulary Practice

A. Definitions. Read the information below. Then match each word in **red** with its definition.

The **legend** of the black Taj Mahal has been around for a long time. According to the story, Shah Jahan wanted a monument for himself. His monument would be similar to the Taj Mahal, but would use black marble. Some believe the monument was never **finished**. Others don't think the story is true.

Shah Jahan **supposedly** wanted to build his monument in a garden across the river from the Taj Mahal. Archeologists searched this area, and some thought they found pieces of black stone. However, these were just white stones that had turned black. They weren't black marble at all.

The archeologists also rebuilt part of a pool that was in the garden, which **couples** like to visit in the evening. When the couples look at the Taj Mahal in the reflection of the pool's water, it sometimes looks black. Perhaps this is where the story came from.

⌃ The reflection of the Taj Mahal at sunset may have started the story of the black Taj Mahal.

1. _____: two people, usually in a relationship
2. _____: ended or completed
3. _____: a story that is passed down from earlier times
4. _____: reportedly; believed to be true

B. Words in Context. Complete each sentence with the correct answer.

1. People often _____ to **express** love.
   a. give flowers   b. hide their emotions

2. When you make a **promise**, you tell someone that you _____ something.
   a. can do   b. will do

3. A **tourist** is someone who _____ .
   a. travels for fun   b. works in a different country

4. The **birth** of a person describes the time he or she _____ .
   a. is born   b. gets married

> **Word Partnership**
> Use **promise** with: (v.) **make** a promise, **keep** a promise, **break** a promise; (adj.) **broken** promise, **empty** promise, **false** promise.

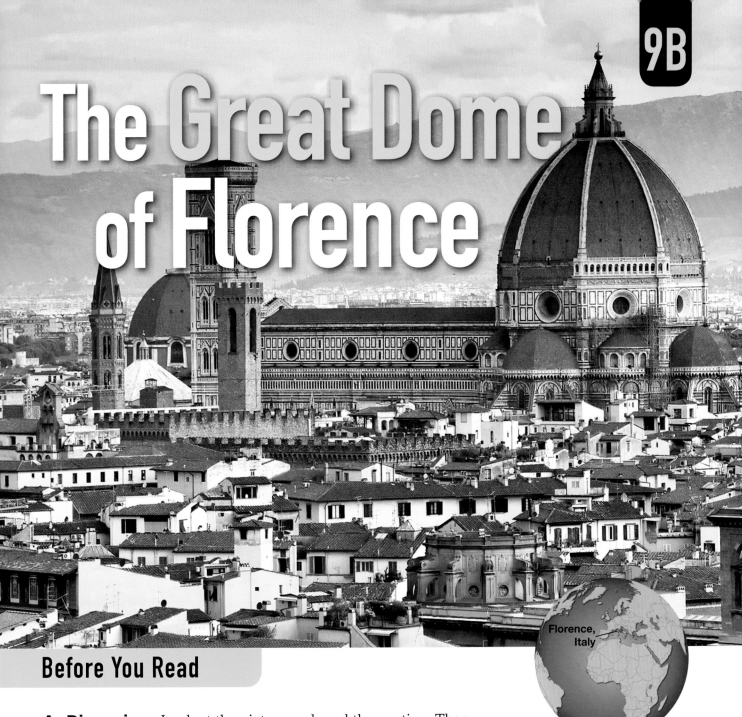

The Great Dome of Florence

Before You Read

A. Discussion. Look at the picture and read the caption. Then discuss the questions below with a partner.

1. What city is the dome above in?
2. What do you think the dome is made of?

B. Predict. What problems do you think the builders of the dome had? Check (✓) your ideas below. Then read the passage on pages 126–127 to check your answers.

The builders couldn't build the dome because they didn't know . . .

☐ what materials to use   ☐ how to raise money

☐ how to support the dome   ☐ how to lift things high up

⌃ Today, the dome of the Basilica di Santa Maria del Fiore is one of Florence's greatest sights. But for over 100 years, the Basilica was unfinished because builders of the time couldn't build the dome.

Florence, Italy

Pantheon
Rome, Italy
ca 130

Hagia Sophia
Istanbul, Turkey
537

Santa Maria del Fiore
Florence, Italy
1471

St. Peter's Basilica
Vatican City
1626

Taj Mahal
Agra, India
ca 1648

Gol Gumbad
Bijapur, India
ca 1656

St. Paul's Cathedral
London, England
1710

U.S. Capitol
Washington, D.C., U.

1 Brunelleschi and the Dome

In 1419, at the beginning of the Renaissance[1] in Italy, a clockmaker
named Filippo Brunelleschi started work on a very difficult **project**.
He was building the dome of Florence's main cathedral,[2] the Basilica
di Santa Maria del Fiore. At 55 meters (180 feet) above ground, it
5 would be the largest dome built since the Pantheon in Rome was
finished 1,500 years before.

After most of the cathedral was built in 1296, many builders tried
to complete the dome. But none could do it. No one knew what
10 **material** to use. Many builders knew how to build concrete[3]
domes. However, the dome in Florence needed to be wider than any
dome ever built. Also, tall buildings of the time **relied** on structures
that **supported** the heavy stone from the outside. The cathedral
didn't have these structures, so a concrete dome was too heavy. It
15 would easily fall. So, the cathedral's roof was left unfinished for over
a hundred years.

Filippo Brunelleschi promised to **solve** all these problems. He said
he would build *two* domes, an inner dome made of stone, and an
outer one made of light bricks.[4] He would use lighter materials as
20 he worked upwards, and would hold it all together with strong rings
made of stone, wood, and iron.

Brunelleschi also had to find a way to **lift** the materials high into the
air. What did he do? He **invented** a new machine to do the job.

Building the dome took 16 years. The crown at the top took another
25 ten. Brunelleschi died a few years later, in 1446. He had done
something no one else could. However, he left no pictures of his
design. So—even today—experts don't fully understand how this
amazing structure was built.

Among the world's
most amazing domes,
the dome in Florence is
second in size only to
St. Peter's Basilica in
Vatican City.

1 The **Renaissance**,
meaning "rebirth," was
a time of great thinkers,
builders, and inventors.

2 A **cathedral** is a kind of
church building, usually
quite big and beautiful.

3 **Concrete** is a hard
construction material
similar to stone.

4 **Bricks** are pieces of baked
clay used for building.

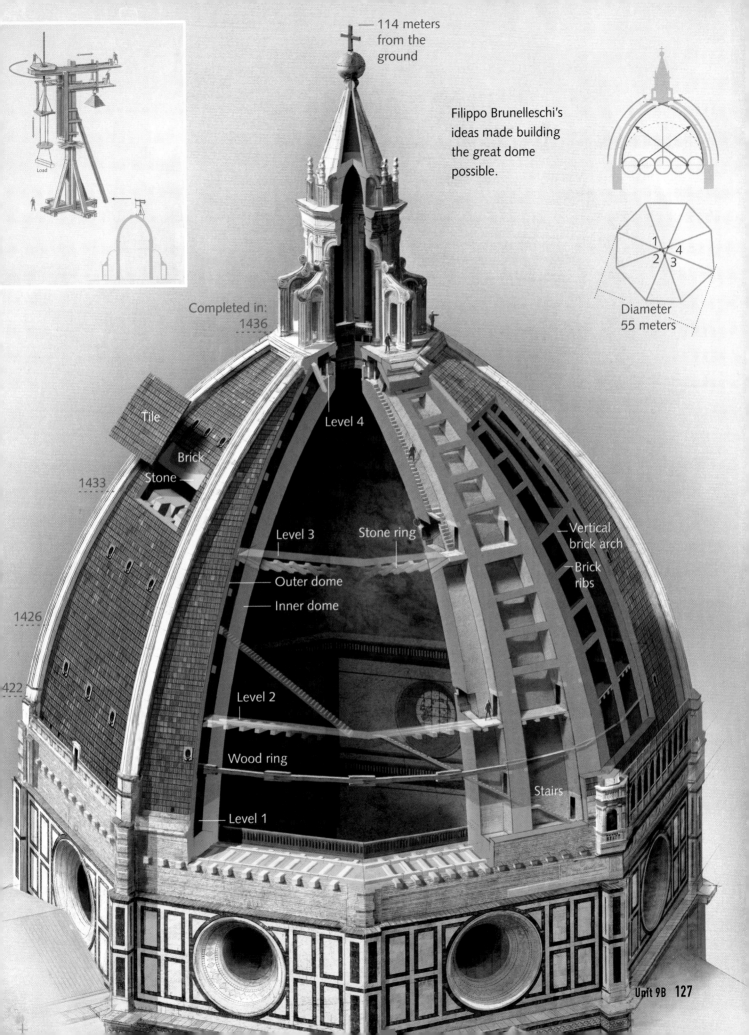

114 meters from the ground

Filippo Brunelleschi's ideas made building the great dome possible.

Load

Completed in:
1436

Tile

Brick

Stone

1433

Level 4

Level 3

Stone ring

Outer dome

Inner dome

Vertical brick arch

Brick ribs

1426

422

Level 2

Wood ring

Level 1

Stairs

Diameter 55 meters

Multiple Choice. Choose the best answer for each question.

Detail
1. Which of the following is NOT given as a reason the dome was difficult to build?
   a. No one had ever built a dome from concrete before.
   b. No one had built such a wide dome before.
   c. The cathedral didn't have structures that could support a dome from the outside.

Purpose
2. What is the purpose of the third paragraph (from line 17)?
   a. to argue another side of an issue
   b. to explain a solution to a problem
   c. to provide background information

Sequence
3. Which of these things happened last?
   a. The Renaissance began.
   b. The cathedral was built.
   c. The dome was completed.

Detail
4. What is true about Filippo Brunelleschi?
   a. He built three domes for the cathedral.
   b. He died before seeing the dome completed.
   c. He invented a machine that lifted things into the air.

Cohesion
5. The following sentence would best be placed at the end of which paragraph? *As a result, there was a large hole in the cathedral's roof.*
   a. paragraph 1
   b. paragraph 2
   c. paragraph 3

Detail
6. Why don't we fully understand how the dome was built?
   a. Brunelleschi didn't leave any pictures of his design.
   b. Some structures are completely covered in concrete.
   c. The dome has been rebuilt many times over the years.

Did You Know?

Inside Florence's cathedral is a 700-year-old clock that places the end of each day—or the 24th hour—at sunset instead of midnight.

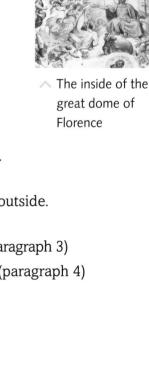

Reading Skill

Recognizing Prepositions

There are different types of prepositions, including those that indicate time (*on Monday*, *for a day*), place (*in India*, *at school*), movement (*to the library*, *into the water*), and possession (*a friend of mine*, *the boy with black hair*). Here are a few examples of English prepositions.

above	at	behind	below	by	during	for	from
in	inside	near	of	on	to	under	with

A. Recognizing. Read the information below. Find and underline all the prepositions.

Tips for Visiting the Great Dome in Florence

- Any visitor to Florence should climb to the top of the cathedral. It's an easy walk up the stairs to the dome area.

- The dome is covered with lovely paintings. Look closely at the walls for graffiti that was made by other tourists. Much of it is over a hundred years old. It gives you an idea of the many people who came before you.

- From the top, you get a great 360-degree view of Florence. You can see many of the famous places in the city from there.

B. Completion. Complete the sentences with the correct prepositions from the box. You can use each preposition more than once. Then look back at the reading to check your answers.

The inside of the great dome of Florence

for	from	in	into	of	with

1. The Renaissance began _____ Italy. (paragraph 1)

2. Filippo Brunelleschi built the dome _____ Florence's main cathedral. (paragraph 1)

3. Buildings _____ that time needed to support heavy stone _____ the outside. (paragraph 2)

4. Brunelleschi planned to hold the dome together _____ strong rings. (paragraph 3)

5. Brunelleschi invented a machine to lift heavy materials _____ the air. (paragraph 4)

6. Brunelleschi died _____ 1446. (paragraph 5)

7. Brunelleschi left no pictures _____ his design. (paragraph 5)

Critical Thinking Discuss with a partner. Which do you think was more difficult to build—the Taj Mahal or the dome of Florence's cathedral? Why?

Unit 9B **129**

Vocabulary Practice

A. Completion. Complete the information below with the correct words in the box. One word is extra.

> design   material   project   rely   supported

Some love it. Others hate it. But it looks like London's Millennium Dome is here to stay. The dome itself is made of a very strong **1.** _____ that is only a millimeter thick. This makes the dome very light. The air inside the dome is heavier than the roof itself. This material is **2.** _____ by twelve towers, one for every hour of the clock. This makes the whole dome look like a big clock from above.

When the dome opened in 2000, many were pleased with the interesting **3.** _____ . But some were unhappy because—for such an expensive **4.** _____ —it had not brought in as many visitors as the builders predicted. Today, the Millennium Dome is better known as the O2 Arena, and is a stadium for music and sporting events.

∧ Designed by architect Richard Rogers, the Millennium Dome is 52 meters tall, each meter representing one week of the year.

B. Words in Context. Complete each sentence with the correct answer.

1. If you **invent** something, you _____ it for the first time.
   a. make   b. use

2. When you **lift** something, you move it to a _____ place.
   a. lower   b. higher

3. Someone who has **solved** a problem has found a way to _____ .
   a. make it bigger   b. end it

4. If you **rely** on someone, you _____ them.
   a. don't believe   b. trust

> **Thesaurus**
> **material** Also look up: (*n.*) *cloth, fabric, textile, matter, substance, stuff, medium*

VIEWING Brunelleschi's Dome

Before You Watch

A. Warm Up. Look at the picture and read the caption. Pay attention to the words in **bold**. You will hear them in the video. Match the words with their definitions below.

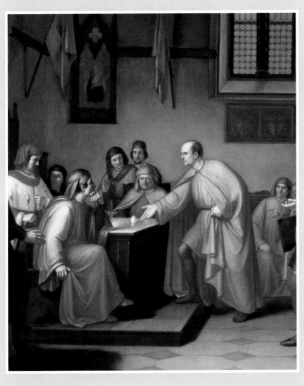

In 1418, a contest was held to solve the problem of the great dome of Florence. Part of the problem was that the cathedral didn't have **arches** to support the dome. Also, the dome's **base** was an **octagon**, so it was not possible to build the usual **semicircle** dome. Filippo Brunelleschi, a master goldsmith,[1] had never trained as an **architect**, but he won the contest and built the dome, using a design that few understand, even today.

---

1 A **master goldsmith** is someone who is very good at working with gold.

1. architect •   • a. a shape that is half of a circle

2. arches •   • b. a shape with eight sides of the same length

3. base •   • c. curved structures that support a wall

4. octagon •   • d. someone who designs buildings

5. semicircle •   • e. the lowest part; the part on which something rests

B. Quiz. What do you know about Florence and its great dome? Answer the questions below. Then check your answers at the bottom of page 132.

1. There are (**163 / 463**) stone steps inside the dome.

2. Around (**400 thousand / four million**) bricks were used to build the dome.

3. When Brunelleschi died, his body was put (**in the dome / under the cathedral**).

4. (**Michelangelo's David / The Venus de Milo**) is a famous statue kept in Florence.

While You Watch

Checking. As you watch the video, check your answers in **Before You Watch B**. Were your ideas correct?

After You Watch

A. Completion. Choose the correct word or phrase to complete each sentence below.

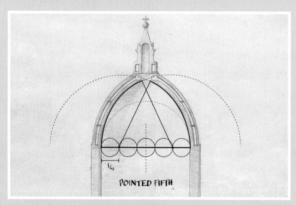

1. The dome needed to be (**eight-** / **sixteen-**)sided.

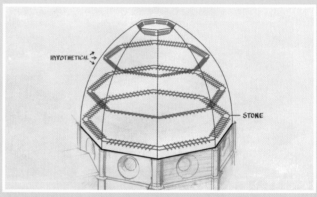

2. The rings in Brunelleschi's design would stop the (**dome from changing shape** / **arches from falling off**).

3. According to the video, Brunelleschi's machines were (**hard to use** / **ahead of their time**).

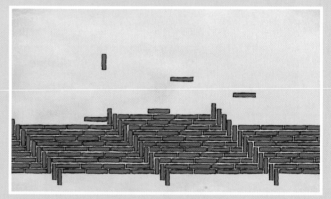

4. The special (**pattern** / **material**) of the dome's bricks helps hold them together.

B. Discuss. Discuss these questions with a partner.

1. Are there any interesting buildings in your city? Do you know why they were built that way?

2. Brunelleschi wasn't trained as an architect, but he was a master goldsmith and clockmaker. Do you think these skills helped him design and build the dome? How?

1. 463; 2. four million; 3. under the cathedral; 4. Michelangelo's David

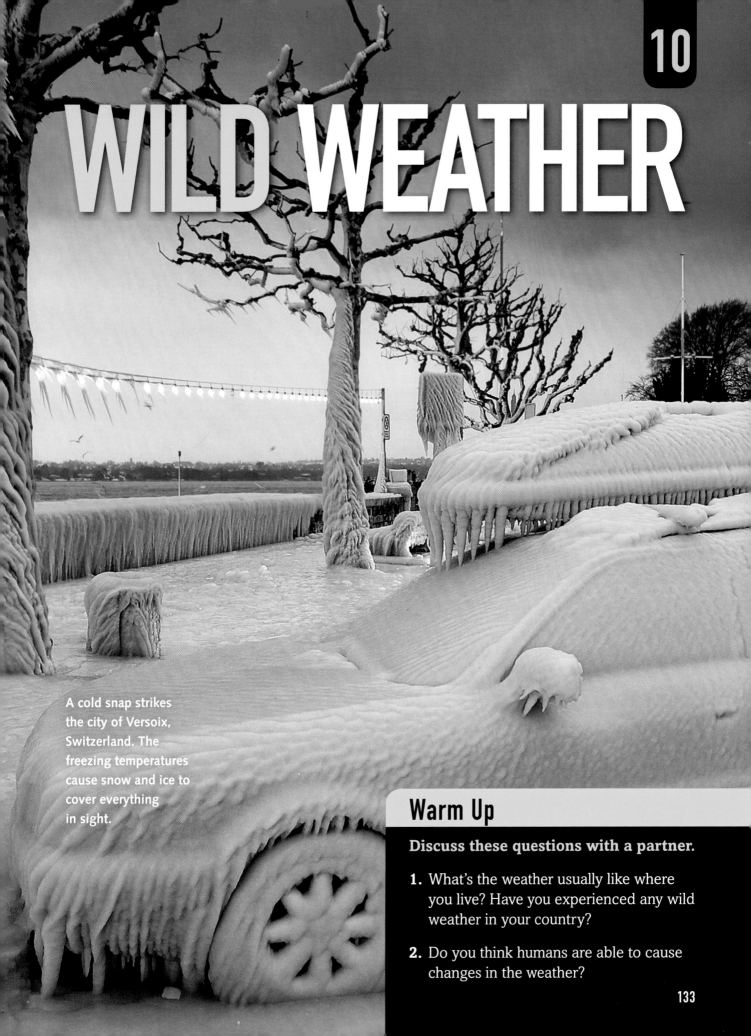

10

WILD WEATHER

A cold snap strikes the city of Versoix, Switzerland. The freezing temperatures cause snow and ice to cover everything in sight.

Warm Up

Discuss these questions with a partner.

1. What's the weather usually like where you live? Have you experienced any wild weather in your country?

2. Do you think humans are able to cause changes in the weather?

133

Before You Read

A. True or False. What do you know about wild weather events? Read the sentences below. Then mark each sentence as true (**T**) or false (**F**).

1. The center of a **hurricane** is called its "head."   **T**   **F**

2. A **drought** can happen when there's no rain.   **T**   **F**

3. The country with the most **tornadoes** is Australia.   **T**   **F**

4. A **heat wave** can happen in any part of the world.   **T**   **F**

5. A "flash" **flood** is sometimes caused by snow melting.   **T**   **F**

B. Skim for the Main Idea. On this page and the next, skim the title, headings, photos, and captions. What is the passage mainly about? Circle **a**, **b**, or **c**. Then read the passage to check your answer.

a. why the U.S. is getting more dangerous storms

b. what scientists are doing to change the weather

c. how the weather is changing around the world

A Warming WORLD

1   One weekend in May 2010, the weather **forecast** for Nashville, Tennessee, U.S.A., predicted 10 centimeters (4 inches) of rain. By Sunday, over 33 centimeters (13 inches) had fallen. Soon the city was flooded. On the roads, cars

5   were covered by the rising water. "We've got buildings running into cars," the news reported as a small building **floated** by. There were 11 deaths that weekend.

Changing Weather

   The weather is changing. Over the last few years, heavy

10   rains have caused floods in Brazil, Pakistan, and Thailand. Droughts have struck Russia and Australia. Heat waves have killed thousands in Europe, and all over the world, hurricanes and tornadoes strike more **frequently** and with greater **force** than ever before. In 2011 alone, **losses** caused by the

15   weather cost the world 150 billion dollars.

⌃ Hurricanes, droughts, tornadoes, and floods are examples of wild weather events. This picture shows the result of a drought, leaving a pond in China completely dried out.

Warmer and Wetter

As more wild weather events happen, a worried world is beginning to ask questions like: *What is going on with the weather? And why?* Many also want to know: *Is this natural, or are we to **blame**?*

20　The answer seems to be: *a little of both*. Wild weather is natural. But most scientists agree human activity has made the Earth warmer. This global warming makes heat waves more likely to **occur**. The higher **temperatures** also cause more water to enter the air. This causes heavier and more frequent rain. Some scientists 25　also believe global warming makes hurricanes and other storms stronger.

This means we're likely to see more wild weather. "[But] we don't have to just stand there and take it," says scientist Michael Oppenheimer. He and other experts say we need to stop the Earth 30　from getting warmer. We also need to be prepared, to do things that will help save lives.

In May 2010, heavy rains caused floods in Nashville, U.S.A. The flood waters covered whole areas of the city, like this parking lot.

Reading Comprehension

Multiple Choice. Choose the best answer for each question.

Main Idea

1. What is the main idea of the reading passage?
   a. There was a deadly flood in Nashville, Tennessee, U.S.A.
   b. Global warming is causing wilder weather events.
   c. Wild weather events are making people very worried.

Purpose

2. What is the purpose of the second paragraph (from line 8)?
   a. to give examples of recent wild weather events
   b. to describe the weather events that occurred in 2011
   c. to predict how the weather will change in a few years

Paraphrase

3. Which of the following is closest in meaning to *What is going on with the weather?* (line 18)?
   a. What will the weather do next?
   b. What was the weather like before?
   c. Why are we having such strange weather?

Reference

4. What does *this* refer to in line 19?
   a. a worried world
   b. the increase in wild weather
   c. deaths caused by wild weather

Vocabulary

5. In line 28, the word *take* could be replaced by _____.
   a. feel good about
   b. do nothing about
   c. find out more about

Inference

6. Which of the following statements would Oppenheimer probably agree with?
   a. It is too late to stop global warming.
   b. Stop global warming, and the weather will get better.
   c. The most important thing, in preparing for wild weather, is to find ways to keep our things safe.

Did You Know?

Lightning is very hot—a flash can heat the air around it to temperatures five times hotter than the surface of the sun.

Identifying Text Types

Each time you encounter a new reading passage, try to determine what type of text it is. Knowing the text type allows you to predict what kind of information the text may contain and how it is organized. This will help you follow it more easily. Here are four of the most common text types.

Narrative texts entertain the reader by telling a story.
Expository texts inform the reader by providing facts and general information.
Technical texts provide information that helps the reader perform a task.
Persuasive texts try to convince the reader to agree with an opinion.

A. Multiple Choice. Look back at the passage on pages 135–136. What kind of text is it? Circle **a**, **b**, **c**, or **d**.

| a. narrative | b. expository | c. technical | d. persuasive |

B. Matching. Read the four paragraphs below. Then match each one to the correct text type.

| a. narrative | b. expository | c. technical | d. persuasive |

1. _____ . . . since floods occur more often than tornadoes or earthquakes. There is a strong chance that you will experience a flood in your lifetime. This is why it's important to protect your home. Everyone should . . .

2. _____ . . . may just save your life. First, go to the safest place possible. This is usually in the basement of your building, if you have one. Next, go to the center of the room and keep away from windows. Stay there until you are sure the tornado …

3. _____ . . . and just as we got to the top of the mountain, it started to rain. There was lightning all around, so we knew we had to find a safe place right away. I wanted to run under a tree, but my friends . . .

4. _____ . . . a cyclone is a collection of thunderstorms. In general, both typhoons and hurricanes are tropical storms, but they occur in different places. Cyclones in the Pacific are called typhoons, and those in the Atlantic are called hurricanes . . .

Critical Thinking Discuss with a partner. How prepared are you for "wild weather"? What are some ways you can be better prepared?

Vocabulary Practice

A. Completion. Choose the correct words to complete the information.

In early 2012, "once-a-century" floods in Ireland left large areas of land underwater. In June, very high **1.** (**losses** / **temperatures**) caused wildfires in Russia. Months later, Hurricane Sandy killed hundreds in North America with **2.** (**losses** / **forecasts**) that cost the country about $150 billion.

Each of these events was dangerous enough on its own. However, in 2013, *all* of these types of weather events **3.** (**blamed** / **occurred**) one after another in Australia. In fact, the country has experienced a huge increase in wild weather events in the past few years, including more **4.** (**frequent** / **floating**) droughts, tornadoes, and heat waves.

Because there is so much wild weather in Australia, more and more scientists are studying its weather patterns to see if they can help make better weather **5.** (**forecasts** / **temperatures**).

B. Words in Context. Complete each sentence with the correct answer.

1. An example of something that **floats** is _____.
   a. a rock   b. a piece of wood

2. The **force** of a tornado refers to its _____.
   a. shape   b. strength

3. If you **blame** someone, you say they _____.
   a. caused something   b. stopped something
     bad to happen   bad from happening

4. Something that happens **frequently** happens _____.
   a. often   b. rarely

> **Word Partnership**
> Use *temperature* with:
> (*adj.*) **high** temperature,
> **low** temperature,
> **average** temperature,
> **daytime** temperature.

A man carries a child through floodwaters in Jakarta, Indonesia

FREAKY FORCES of Nature

Before You Read

A. Discussion. Look at the picture above and read the caption. Then discuss these questions with a partner.

1. What other strange weather events have you heard of? Can you explain why they happen?

2. Do you know any interesting stories about strange weather?

B. Skim. Quickly skim the reading passage on page 141. Match the headings below to the correct paragraphs in the passage. One heading is extra.

a. Tornadoes of Fire
b. Floods Rising!
c. Great Balls of Ice!
d. Strange Rain!

△ A giant cloud of dust, called a *haboob*, quickly covers the city of Phoenix, Arizona, U.S.A. The wall of dust is 1,500 meters (5,000 feet) tall and 160 kilometers (100 miles) long. It is just one of many strange weather events seen on Earth.

When Weird Weather Strikes

Most of us know about fires, hurricanes, droughts, and floods. But from time to time, Mother Nature[1] surprises us, and **delivers** a weather event that is really **weird**. Here are some examples of truly weird weather.

1. _____: One day in 2005, residents[2] of a small town in Serbia looked out their windows and saw an unusual sight. It was raining frogs! Without any **warning**, they found their streets filling with the little jumping creatures. "There were thousands of them," one resident told a **local** newspaper. "I thought perhaps a plane carrying frogs had exploded,"[3] said another. Scientists think a tornado passed over a lake. It sucked up animals that lived there. The frogs were carried into the air. Then they were **dropped** in the Serbian town, far away.

2. _____: As if tornadoes aren't dangerous enough, some of them can **actually** be made of fire. When a wildfire reaches very high temperatures, it causes the air to become hot and to rise. Cooler air **rushes** in to replace the hot air. This creates strong winds. These winds suck up burning plants and even the fire itself. When this happens, like it did on March 14, 2014, in Denver, Colorado, U.S.A., a tornado of fire is produced. This tornado can become 15 meters (50 feet) wide and grow as tall as a 40-story building.

3. _____: In 1942, hundreds of thousand-year-old skeletons were found under the ice of Lake Roopkund in the Himalayas. Many had holes in their skulls. But they weren't hurt in any other way. Scientists thought the people must have been hit from above. But for years, the cause of their deaths was a mystery.
Today, scientists think these people were killed by giant hailstones—balls of ice. Hailstones form when raindrops high in the sky turn into pieces of ice. The ice pieces **increase** in size until the wind cannot hold them up. This results in hailstones falling to the ground, often at speeds of over 160 kilometers (100 miles) an hour. For the unlucky people at Lake Roopkund, there was nowhere to run. They were all killed by the hailstones.

---

1 **Mother Nature** is a term used to describe nature as if it were a woman.

2 A **resident** is a person who lives in a certain place.

3 If something **explodes** (e.g., a bomb), it suddenly breaks apart with parts flying outward.

A tornado of fire is formed by strong winds in a forest fire.

Multiple Choice. Choose the best answer for each question.

Gist

1. Another title for this reading could be _____.
   a. Unusual Tornadoes
   b. Humans vs. Nature
   c. Strange Weather

Vocabulary

2. The words *sucked up* in line 13 could be replaced with _____.
   a. lifted
   b. used
   c. blew

Detail

3. What is probably true about the frogs that rained down in Serbia?
   a. They fell out of an airplane that exploded.
   b. A tornado took them from a lake and dropped them over the town.
   c. They were carried away as babies, grew in the clouds, and then fell down to Earth.

Reference

4. The word *this* in line 22 refers to the moment when _____.
   a. a wildfire grows really big
   b. rushing winds suck up the fire
   c. the tornado of fire becomes 15 meters wide

Cohesion

5. The following sentence would best be placed at the end of which paragraph? *This makes them very dangerous.*
   a. paragraph 1 (from line 1)
   b. paragraph 2 (from line 6)
   c. paragraph 3 (from line 16)

Detail

6. What happens when little pieces of ice move around in the wind?
   a. They become bigger.
   b. They become raindrops.
   c. They fall to the ground as snow.

Did You Know?

In November 2007, residents in Changsha, China, were surprised when they found a street filled with "fish rain." They later found out it never really rained fish. The fish probably fell off a truck.

Identifying Cause and Effect

Identifying causes and effects in a passage can help you see how events change other events. To identify causes and effects, you can often look out for words like *cause, result, create,* and *produce*.

Sometimes causes and effects are described without using these words. When two events in a passage seem to be connected, ask yourself: *Which event occurred first? Did it change the event that follows?*

A. Scan. Look back at the reading on page 141. Find examples of causes and effects in the passage. Underline the causes and circle the effects.

B. Matching. Look at the chart below. Match the causes on the left with the effects on the right.

Causes	Effects
1. a tornado passes over a lake	a. hundreds of people died
2. a wildfire reaches high temperatures	b. hail falls to the ground
3. cool air rushes into a wildfire	c. strong winds are created
4. wildfire winds suck up the fire itself	d. the air becomes hot and rises
5. pieces of ice in the air grow too big	e. frogs are lifted into the air
6. hailstones fell from the sky	f. a tornado of fire is produced

Critical Thinking Discuss with a partner. What would you do if you were caught in a hailstorm? Saw a tornado of fire? Got rained on by frogs?

A fire tornado comes dangerously close to people's homes in California, in the U.S.

Vocabulary Practice

A. Completion. Complete the information with the words from the box. One word is extra.

| actually | increase | local | rushing | warning | weird |

Mystery Waves

Imagine this: You are out at sea, relaxing on a boat. It's a beautiful day. No rain is falling, and the winds are calm. All at once, something very **1.** _____ happens. Out of nowhere, you see a wall of water ten stories tall **2.** _____ toward you.

This is known as a *rogue wave*, also called a *freak wave*. Some people mistake them for tsunamis, but they are **3.** _____ very different. Tsunamis start out very small in the open ocean, and only **4.** _____ in speed and height as they get close to the coast. When a tsunami is coming, the water will often seem to be sucked back into the ocean. There is usually no **5.** _____ before a rogue wave strikes. This kind of wave can appear even in the best of weather.

Scientists aren't sure what causes these waves. In fact, as recently as 15 years ago, people thought these waves didn't really exist. But scientists now know they are very real—and very dangerous—even to the largest ships.

B. Words in Context. Complete each sentence with the correct answer.

1. If something **drops**, it _____ .
   a. falls to the ground   b. moves up into the air

2. You are a **local** in the city, you _____ .
   a. grew up in   b. just moved to

3. If you describe a movie as **weird**, you think it is _____ .
   a. funny   b. strange

4. When you **deliver** a letter, you usually _____ someone.
   a. bring it to   b. get it from

> **Usage**
> *Drop* vs. *fall*
> Both *fall* and *drop* mean "to move downward quickly". However, we use *drop* when someone or something holds an object and lets it go, e.g., *I **fell** down the stairs.* vs. *I **dropped** my phone on the street.*

VIEWING Storm of the Century

Before You Watch

Warm Up. Look at the picture and read the caption.
Then answer the questions below. Discuss your ideas with a partner.

∧ Often, tropical storms with heavy rain and strong winds start in the Atlantic Ocean. When a tropical storm reaches wind speeds of 63 kilometers per hour (39 miles per hour), it is given a name, like Sandy, Dolly, or Hugo. When it gains wind speeds of 119 kilometers per hour (74 miles per hour), it is no longer a tropical storm; it is now called a *hurricane*.

The worst hurricane in U.S. history was the Great Galveston Hurricane of 1900, which killed between 8,000 and 12,000 people. That day, floodwaters came up to almost five meters. Since then, there hadn't been a storm as bad, until the arrival of what many are now calling "the storm of the century."

1. Does your country experience big storms? When was the last big weather event in your country?
2. The video is about Hurricane Katrina, which hit New Orleans in the U.S., in 2005. Have you heard of this hurricane? If so, what do you know about it?

While You Watch

A. Checking. Are your ideas from **Before You Watch** talked about in the video?

B. Multiple Choice. As you watch the video, choose the correct answer for each question below.

1. The video says that in recent years there were _____ as many strong storms.

   a. twice   b. three times   c. four times

2. Scientists use images that show _____ to see the power of the storm.

   a. heat   b. waves   c. losses

3. Mayfield thinks that after people see what the storm did, they should _____.

   a. want to help stop global warming
   b. find a new place to live, away from the sea
   c. buy better weather-prediction machines

After You Watch

A. Completion. Complete the sentences below using the numbers in the box.

1	1	2	2	3

1. Katrina's winds reached about _____ hundred eighty kilometers per hour.
2. Over a few days, _____ million people lost their homes to the floods.
3. Katrina took almost _____ thousand lives.
4. Water levels in Mayfield's neighborhood rose to almost _____ meters.
5. The losses caused by Katrina cost the U.S. about _____ hundred billion dollars.

B. Discuss. Discuss these questions with a partner.

1. The video says that after Katrina, "for many, things will never be the same." What do you think this means?
2. Why do you think some tropical storms are given names? Do you think it's a good idea?

❮ Rescue workers in a boat help a woman leave her flooded home.

11

Giants of the Past

Millions of years ago, super-sized creatures like the dinosaurs walked the Earth and swam the seas. But they are all gone now.

Warm Up

Discuss these questions with a partner.

1. Do you know of any animals that don't exist anymore?

2. What do you think caused these animals to die out?

147

The MAMMOTH'S Tale

Before You Read

Lyuba is the best-preserved mammoth mummy in the world.

A. Matching. Tens of thousands of years ago, woolly mammoths walked the Earth. These creatures were related to today's elephants. Read the information below. Then match the words in **bold** to their definitions.

MAMMOTH
- Long, thick hair
- Long, curved **tusks**
- Lived during the **Ice Age** in Siberia and North America
- Became **extinct** 4,000 years ago

ELEPHANT
- Thick skin but very little hair
- Short, straight tusks
- 470,000 elephants living today, mainly in hot places like India and Africa

1. _____: no longer existing or living

2. _____: a time when ice covered much of the Earth

3. _____: long, pointed teeth used to fight or to find food

B. Predict. Look at the pictures and captions on this page and the next. What do you think happened to the mammoth after it was found? Discuss with a partner. Then read the passage to check your ideas.

1 *Imagine finding a body that had been lost for 40,000 years . . .*

The strange animal in the ice looked like it was sleeping. Ten-year-old Kostia Khudi and his brother had never seen anything like it before. But they had heard stories of the
5 *mamont*. It was an imaginary animal that lived in the ice-filled blackness of the Siberian underworld.[1] Their father, a reindeer herder[2] named Yuri Khudi, went to ask a friend for advice.[3] But when he returned, the body had **vanished**.

Yuri soon found the animal's body **leaning against** a store in
10 a nearby town. While he was away, his cousin had sold it to the store owner. Dogs had eaten part of the tail and ear, but it was still in "as close to **perfect** condition as you can imagine," says scientist Daniel Fisher. The police came to help. The body was taken by helicopter to a museum.[4] The animal was a baby
15 mammoth from the Ice Age. It was female, so the scientists named it after Yuri's wife.

From Siberia, the mammoth was sent to the Netherlands and Japan. Scientists there studied it more closely. **Detailed** studies of her teeth and tusks showed she was just one month old when
20 she died. **Ongoing** research has also shown us the **sequence** of events that led to her death. Lyuba fell and died near a muddy river. The mud helped keep her body frozen until she was found, 40,000 years later. Scientists hope that **further** studies will help explain how mammoths, like Lyuba lived. They also want to
25 know why mammoths became extinct.

⌃ Lyuba died when she fell into wet mud near a river.

⌃ The ground froze. It kept Lyuba's body whole.

⌃ In 2006, melting caused Lyuba's body to wash free.

---

1 The **underworld** is an underground world, where some people believe the dead go.

2 A **herder** looks after a large group of animals.

3 If you ask someone for **advice**, you ask them what they think you should do in a particular situation.

4 A **museum** is a place where old things are kept on display.

Reading Comprehension

Multiple Choice. Choose the best answer for each question.

Gist

1. The passage is mainly about _____ .
   a. animals that are now extinct
   b. an important discovery
   c. what life was like for a mammoth named Lyuba

Sequence

2. Which of the following happened first?
   a. Yuri's cousin sold the mammoth to a store owner.
   b. Lyuba's body was taken to a museum.
   c. The police arrived to take Lyuba's body away.

Purpose

3. What is the purpose of the second paragraph (from line 9)?
   a. to describe the condition of Lyuba when she was found
   b. to describe the difficulties of studying a mammoth's body
   c. to describe how Lyuba was found again and taken to a
      safe place

Reference

4. The word *it* (line 11) refers to the mammoth's _____ .
   a. ear
   b. tail
   c. body

Inference

5. Which of the following can be inferred from the passage?
   a. Yuri's wife's name was Lyuba.
   b. The mammoth died when the Ice Age ended.
   c. Yuri's cousin didn't know what the mammoth
      was when he sold it.

Detail

6. How did Lyuba die?
   a. Dogs killed her.
   b. Hunters killed her.
   c. She died when she fell.

Did You Know?

Some scientists think mammoths died out because the Earth became too warm and they couldn't find enough food. Others think humans hunted them to extinction.

Recognizing Active and Passive Sentences

Reading passages often include a mix of active and passive sentences. In active sentences, *the subject* is the **doer** of the action (the verb). In passive sentences, *the subject* is the **receiver** of the action. Look at these examples and notice how passive sentences are formed.

Active	Passive (*be* + past participle)
The boys <u>found</u> a mammoth.	*A mammoth* <u>was found</u> (by the boys).
The man's cousin <u>had sold</u> it.	*It* <u>had been sold</u> (by the man's cousin).
Scientists <u>will study</u> it.	*It* <u>will be studied</u> (by scientists).

A. Analyzing. Read the sentences below. Circle the subject of each sentence. Then mark each as active (**A**) or passive (**P**).

Example: (People) found 158 paintings in a
cave in France.   Ⓐ   P

1. These pictures were painted by early humans.   **A**   **P**
2. The paintings show early man and mammoths.   **A**   **P**
3. Mammoth tusks were used to make tools.   **A**   **P**
4. These tools were used by early man to hunt.   **A**   **P**
5. People today search for more mammoth tusks.   **A**   **P**

B. Completion. Are these sentences active or passive? Choose the correct word or phrase to complete each sentence. Then check your answers on page 149.

1. Dogs (**had eaten / had been eaten**) part of the tail.
2. The body (**took / was taken**) by helicopter to a museum.
3. The mammoth (**sent / was sent**) to the Netherlands.
4. Further studies (**will explain / will be explained**) how mammoths lived and died.

Critical Thinking Discuss with a partner. Some scientists want to bring extinct animals, like mammoths, back to life. Do you think they should? Why or why not?

∧ The tusk of a full-grown mammoth could grow as long as 5.2 meters (17 feet).

Vocabulary Practice

A. Completion. Complete the information below using the correct word or phrase.

Close your eyes. Can you **1. (lean against / imagine)** a crocodile so big that it eats dinosaurs? Scientists say such a crocodile really did live 110 million years ago in Africa, but it **2. (vanished / imagined)** from Earth even before the dinosaurs became extinct. They call it "SuperCroc."

In 2000, Paul Sereno and his team found some SuperCroc bones in the Sahara Desert. After some **3. (perfect / further)** searching, they had enough bones to make up 50 percent of SuperCroc's skeleton.

From their work, the scientists learned many **4. (sequences / details)** about SuperCroc's life. For example, they now know it grew to about 8,000 kilograms (17,600 pounds) and that its strong jaws and strong teeth were **5. (ongoing / perfect)** for catching and holding prey. The bones are now in museums, so people can learn about this amazing animal.

∧ Paleontologist Paul Sereno studies dinosaurs and other creatures of the past. The SuperCroc fossils he discovered belong to a crocodile skeleton measuring 12 meters (40 feet) in length.

B. Words in Context. Complete each sentence with the correct answer.

1. If something is **ongoing**, it is _____.
   a. finished   b. not finished

2. When you **lean against** a wall, you bend your body _____ it.
   a. toward   b. away from

3. If something is **perfect**, you probably want to _____.
   a. keep it the way it is   b. change it

4. A **sequence** of events refers to a number of events that come _____.
   a. one after another   b. at the same time

> **Usage**
> The word **further** means "more" or "additional." The word **farther**, however, usually refers to a greater distance.

Sea Monsters

A *Tylosaurus* reaches for a shark with its great jaws.

Before You Read

A. Labeling. Read the information below. Then label the picture above with the numbers in **bold**. Write **1–5** in the circles.

At 14 meters (45 feet) long, *Tylosaurus* was one of the biggest sea monsters[1] of all time. By looking at fossils,[2] scientists know that *Tylosaurus* had great **1. jaws** and big **2. teeth**. Studies of its **3. stomach** contents show it ate fish, seabirds, and even sharks. It used its long **4. tail** to push itself through the water and its two shorter **5. fins** to change direction. *Tylosaurus* was not related to the dinosaurs, but it lived and became extinct around the same time.

1 The word *monster* usually refers to a large, frightening creature.

2 **Fossils** are the hard remains of animals or plants that lived millions of years ago.

B. Predict. Look quickly at the headings, pictures, and captions on pages 154–155. Answer the questions below. Then read the passage to check your answers.

1. How many "giants of the sea" does the passage mention?

2. What do you think was unusual about each creature?

Monsters of the Deep

Sea monsters are not just imaginary creatures. Millions of years ago, real monsters did actually live on Earth.

Today, scientists use fossils to help them **figure out** what these monsters were like. The fossils can help us understand some of the animals' unusual **characteristics**. After studying the fossils, the scientists can make very detailed pictures of these animals. So now, we can all see what they looked like.

Eyes in the Dark

Temnodontosaurus was **definitely** an unusual animal. Its name means "cutting-tooth lizard," and with good reason—it had very big teeth. It also had some of the largest eyes in nature. They were over 25 centimeters (10 inches) across! With such big eyes, *Temnodontosaurus* could easily find its food in the dark water.

Terror of the Deep

Kronosaurus—the "Kronos lizard"—lived in the seas that covered Australia. But it probably used its fins to climb out of the water and lay its eggs on land. Its head was two meters (seven feet) long. Its teeth were as big as bananas! The main **function** of strong jaws and teeth like these was to catch smaller animals. In fact, *Kronosaurus* was one of the most dangerous **predators** of all time.

The Stalker[1]

Known as the "lord of the seas," *Thalassomedon* was a large sea monster with a very long neck. It also had a special **means** of catching fish: It carried stones in its stomach! These helped keep the largest part of its body and tail down in the dark water. Meanwhile, its long neck slowly **rose** up toward the fish. The fish didn't have a **chance** to get away from *Thalassomedon*. They didn't see the sea monster until it was too late!

---

1 To **stalk** someone or something is to follow slowly and quietly.

Thalassomedon

Temnodontosaurus

Kronosaurus

Reading Comprehension

Multiple Choice. Choose the best answer for each question.

Purpose

1. What is the purpose of the reading passage?
   a. to describe the three most dangerous predators of all time
   b. to describe how the fossils of three sea animals were found
   c. to describe three sea animals from the past with unusual characteristics

Vocabulary

2. The phrase *with good reason* (lines 12–13) could be replaced with _____.
   a. and it was smart
   b. as will be explained
   c. this was useful because

Detail

3. Which of these sentences about *Kronosaurus* is NOT true?
   a. Its teeth were very large.
   b. It stayed in the water all the time.
   c. It was a very dangerous predator.

Reference

4. The word *these* in line 29 refers to _____.
   a. fish
   b. stones
   c. ways to catch fish

Detail

5. What is unusual about *Thalassomedon*?
   a. It laid its eggs on land.
   b. It had very large eyes.
   c. It had a very long neck.

Inference

6. Why did the fish not have a chance to get away from *Thalassomedon*?
   a. The fish were very slow swimmers.
   b. The fish thought *Thalassomedon* was friendly.
   c. The fish didn't see *Thalassomedon* as it came near.

Did You Know?

Kronosaurus was the largest sea reptile that ever lived.

Organizing Information in a Chart

One useful way to organize information is to write out important details in a chart. A chart can be a good way to "see" the information we want to compare or remember.

A. Completion. What do you know about these animals? How are they the same or different? Complete the chart with the animal names from the box.

crocodile	elephant	*Kronosaurus*	mammoth	shark	*Temnodontosaurus*	whale

	lives on land	lives in water
Living now		
Extinct		

B. Completion. Complete the chart below using information from the passage on page 154. Write one word in each space.

	Temnodontosaurus	*Kronosaurus*	*Thalassomedon*
Meaning of name	"cutting-_____ lizard"	"Kronos _____"	"lord of the _____"
Unusual characteristics	had very large _____ and _____	had teeth the size of _____	had a very long _____ and _____ in its stomach
Special abilities	could easily see its _____ in the dark water	could _____ smaller animals with its strong _____	was able to get close to _____ without being seen

Critical Thinking Discuss with a partner. In what ways are the three creatures in **B** the same? How are they different?

Vocabulary Practice

A. Completion. Complete the information using the correct form of words from the box. One word is extra.

| chance | characteristic | definitely | figure out | function | means | predator | rise |

For hundreds of years, people have heard reports of monsters that **1.** _____ out of the sea to attack ships. Many people now think these "monsters" were probably giant squid.

Giant squid share many of the same **2.** _____ as other squid. But they are much larger—up to 13 meters (43 feet) in length. They also have the largest eyes of any animal in the world. This helps them catch deep-sea fish.

Their only **3.** _____ are some kinds of whales. When it is attacked, the giant squid has a very clever **4.** _____ of getting away. It shoots dark ink into the water. The whale can't see, so the squid has a **5.** _____ to swim away.

∧ Squid have ten long sticky arms that they use to catch food.

For years, scientists were unable to catch a giant squid on film. But they did find squid body parts in the stomachs of whales. The scientists were able to use these to **6.** _____ how big the squid was. The first photos of a live giant squid were taken in 2004. It is **7.** _____ as monstrous as people believed!

B. Definitions. Use words from the box in **A** to complete the definitions below.

1. Features that are usual for someone or something are called _____ .

2. Your _____ of doing something are your ways of doing it.

3. If there is a _____ of something, there is a possibility it will happen.

4. The _____ of an object is how it is meant to be used.

> **Usage**
> Use **probably** to say something is likely. Use **definitely** if you are sure about something, and **possibly** if there is just a chance something is true or will happen.

VIEWING Days of the Dinosaurs

Before You Watch

Discuss. Look at the picture and read the caption.
Can you name any other dinosaurs? What do you know about them?
Discuss the questions below with a partner.

< The word *dinosaur* means "great lizard"—it was once believed that all dinosaurs were simply giant lizards. Scientists have since found that many dinosaurs also had characteristics similar to those of other animals.

For example, *sauropods* (the long-necked creatures pictured here) walked on four legs but were able to stand on two, like elephants. They also traveled in family groups just like elephants. They had claws[1] and hollow[2] bones like birds.

---

1 **Claws** are sharp, curved structures at the end of animals' toes.
2 If something is **hollow**, it is empty inside.

1. What did dinosaurs look like? Describe some dinosaurs.
2. What do you think *sauropods* ate? What did other dinosaurs eat?
3. Did dinosaurs lay eggs?
4. What modern animal do you think dinosaurs are like?
5. How did the dinosaurs die out?
6. How do you think scientists today learn about dinosaurs?

While You Watch

A. Checking. As you watch the video, check your answers in **Before You Watch**. Were your ideas correct?

B. Completion. As you watch, choose the correct word or phrase from the video to complete each sentence.

1. The scientists dig for (**fossilized bones / dinosaur eggs**).

2. The smallest dinosaur was less than (**one meter long / one kilogram**).

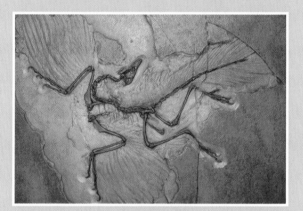

3. Dinosaurs likely died out because the planet was too (**hot and wet / cold and dark**).

4. Scientists believe dinosaurs may be related to the (**birds / snakes**) living today.

After You Watch

A. True or False. Read the sentences below. Then mark each sentence as true (**T**) or false (**F**).

1. *Jobaria* ate meat.	**T**	**F**
2. *Jobaria* was longer than a city bus.	**T**	**F**
3. Most dinosaurs laid eggs.	**T**	**F**
4. Some dinosaurs lived in groups.	**T**	**F**
5. Scientists now know why dinosaurs went extinct.	**T**	**F**

B. Discuss. Discuss these questions with a partner.

1. In the video, the narrator compares the time since the moment dinosaurs first appeared to a single day. What is he trying to say?

2. Why do you think people like to watch movies and read stories about creatures from the past, like dinosaurs and mammoths?

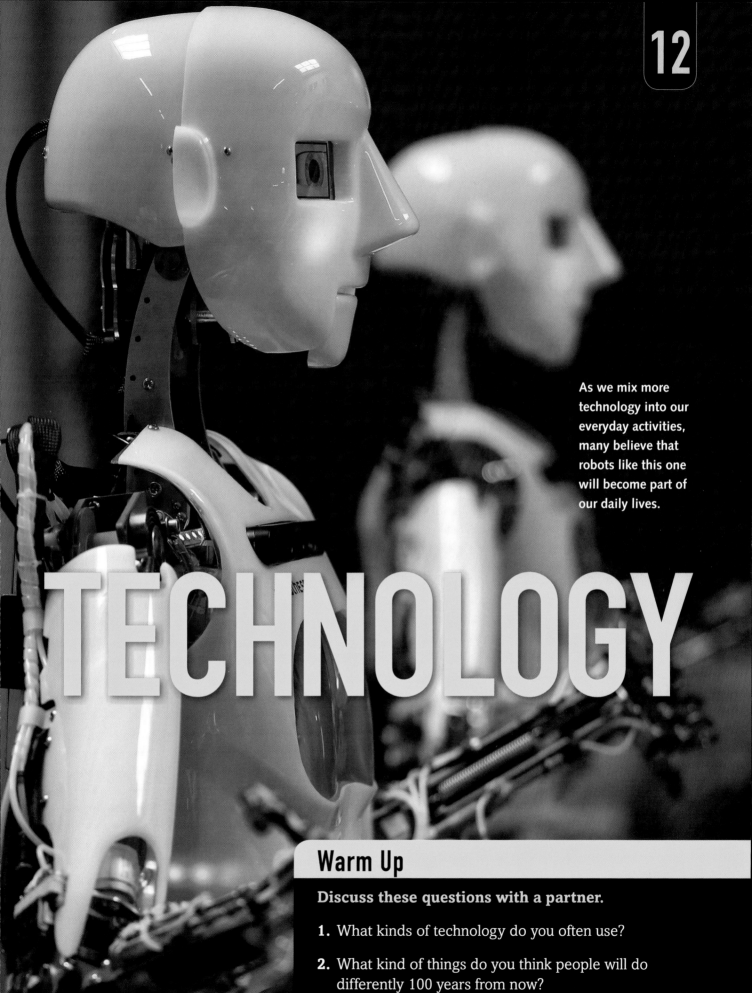

12

As we mix more technology into our everyday activities, many believe that robots like this one will become part of our daily lives.

TECHNOLOGY

Warm Up

Discuss these questions with a partner.

1. What kinds of technology do you often use?

2. What kind of things do you think people will do differently 100 years from now?

Robot helpers for the home and mini-soccer players are just some examples of the robots being built today.

Before You Read

A. Discuss. What can robots do that humans can't? What can humans do that robots can't? Use the words and phrases from the box, and add your own ideas.

climb stairs	feel emotions	fight fires
jump	play soccer	run
take care of people	drive cars	walk on water
walk up walls	work in space	write poems

B. Scan. Look quickly at the reading. Which of the things above are mentioned in the reading? Do you think today's robots can do them? Read the passage to check your ideas.

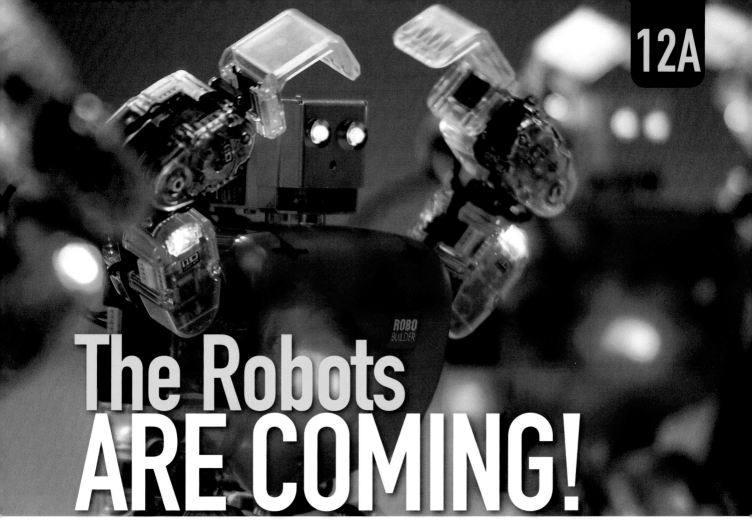

The Robots ARE COMING!

1　The year is 2045. A goal is scored at the soccer World Cup. Not by a human player, but by a robot. *A robot? Is that possible?* Many scientists believe it is. In fact, there are already robots that can play soccer. Of course, today's robots don't just play **sports**. Today's
5　scientists are working on robots with various skills. For example, it is very possible that robots will soon help take care of children or the elderly,[1] or do dangerous jobs such as fighting fires.

　When people started making robots, they were made to do just **simple** things, mainly in **factories**. Since then, however, robots have
10　changed a lot. Early robots were **operated** by humans. Today's robots function on their own. Some can only move around a little, like robot vacuum cleaners,[2] but others, such as Honda's ASIMO, can do much more. He can run, climb stairs, dance, and yes, even play soccer.

　Then there are robots designed to be like humans. These robots have
15　faces and can show emotions. Such robots can learn new things, and show us how they "feel." Actroid-DER—a social robot—looks so human, she sometimes makes people feel **uncomfortable**.

1　Someone who is **elderly** is old.
2　A **vacuum cleaner** is a machine that cleans the floor by sucking up dirt.

Animal-bots

Scientists aren't just building humanlike robots. They are also making
robots that look and act like animals.

At NASA, scientists are making a robot snake. They think it's a good
alternative to vehicles with wheels. These snake-bots can enter
holes and move over **rough** ground. They might one day help
scientists look for **signs** of life on Mars. Other animal robots include
the frog-bot, which can jump over objects, and the sticky-bot, which
can walk up walls. There's even a robot called Water Runner that can
walk on water.

But can a robot soccer team ever operate all on their own, or play
as well as a human team? Many robot scientists definitely think so.
Anything is possible. One day, they may even be world champions!

⌄ Among the robots of today
are Honda's ASIMO (top left),
the NASA snake-bot (bottom left),
and Actroid-DER—the social
robot (right).

Reading Comprehension

Multiple Choice. Choose the best answer for each question.

Gist

1. The passage is mainly about _____.
  a. things robots can do
  b. why people need robots
  c. how to make your own robot

Purpose

2. What is the purpose of the second paragraph (from line 8)?
  a. to describe how the earliest robots were used in factories
  b. to explain how today's robots are different from early robots
  c. to explain why early robots could not do things by themselves

Detail

3. Which robot is able to show its feelings?
  a. ASIMO
  b. Actroid-DER
  c. Water Runner

Reference

4. The word *they* (line 23) refers to _____.
  a. vehicles
  b. wheels
  c. snake-bots

Detail

5. Which of the following robots would best be able to move over a large rock in its path?
  a. A frog-bot
  b. Actroid-DER
  c. Water Runner

Inference

6. Which statement would the author probably agree with?
  a. A frog-bot can do more things than a sticky-bot.
  b. Robots should not have to do difficult jobs for humans.
  c. There could be robot soccer players that think for themselves in the World Cup by 2045.

Did You Know?

Leonardo da Vinci drew up plans for a humanlike machine in 1495. In 2009, artists made this model of Leonardo's design.

Supporting Ideas with Examples

Writers often use examples to support their ideas or help explain difficult concepts. Words that show where examples are in a text include *for instance*, *for example*, *like*, and *such as*.

A. Completion. Look back at paragraphs 1 and 2 of the passage on pages 163–164. Find and write the example of each thing below. (Look out for words that show where the examples are.)

1. a sport that robots can play   _____
2. a skill other than a sport   _____
3. a dangerous job   _____
4. a type of robot that moves around a little   _____
5. a robot that does more than move around   _____

B. Completion. Choose examples from the box to complete the information below.

> a. he could be seen at the Henry Ford Museum
> b. "I am Elektro" and "My brain is bigger than yours."
> c. sitting, barking, and begging for food
> d. he could walk, talk, and move his arms and legs

∧ Elektro is 2.1 meters (7 feet) tall and weighs 120 kilograms (265 pounds).

One of the first humanlike robots was Elektro. Built between 1937 and 1939, he could do many basic human actions. For example, **1.** _____ . He was first seen at the New York World's Fair in 1939, with Sparko, a robot dog that could do tricks, such as **2.** _____ . In 1992, a dance band recorded a song that used some things Elektro once said, like, **3.** _____ . Elektro's usual home is at the Mansfield Memorial Museum in Ohio, U.S.A, but he often travels to other museums. For instance, in 2013, **4.** _____ .

Critical Thinking Discuss with a partner. Some people fear that one day robots will completely replace other human beings in our lives. Do you think this could happen? What jobs do you think robots could do better than humans? Are there things only humans can do?

Vocabulary Practice

A. Completion. Complete the information using words from the box. One word is extra.

| alternative   operate   rough   simple   uncomfortable |

Some robots today are learning to walk. Putting one foot in front of the other is usually so **1.** _____ that a child can do it. But walking is difficult for robots, and nearly impossible over **2.** _____ ground. Researchers are working to help robots walk better by giving them machine parts that act like human bones and muscles.

A robot pet provides a(n) **3.** _____ to keeping a real animal. It moves, cries, senses your movements, and can even learn basic words. But some people are **4.** _____ with robot pets. They worry that robot pets could replace contact with real animals or even other humans.

∧ A robot seal named Paro helps elderly people feel better. Paro can play with people and even learn from them.

B. Words in Context. Complete each sentence with the correct answer.

1. _____ are examples of **sports**.

   a. Basketball and tennis   b. Balls and nets

2. A **factory** is a place where products are _____.

   a. made   b. sold

3. A **sign** of something _____.

   a. is a picture in your mind   b. shows that it exists

4. If you **operate** a machine, you _____ it.

   a. use   b. fix

> **Word Partnership**
> Use **operate** with: (*n.*) operate a **machine**, operate a **business**, operate a **company**.

∧ An artist's idea of
what a home in the
future might look like

Before You Read

A. Predict. Look at the pictures on this page and the next, and
read the captions. Then answer the questions below.

1. What do you think the passage will say about the future?

2. What other things do you think will be different in the future?

B. Skim. Skim the passage on page 169. Check (✓) the topics the
author makes predictions about. Then read the whole passage to
check your answers. Were your ideas in **A** correct?

☐ health   ☐ entertainment   ☐ clothing

☐ food   ☐ transportation   ☐ work

How Will We Live in 2035?

1   Welcome to life in the **future**!

You get up in the morning and look into the **mirror**. You've just had an anti-aging **treatment**, so your face looks youthful. In 2035, many people your age could live to be 150, so at 60,
5   you're not old at all.

Science has also found amazing ways to keep people healthy. There are nanotechnology[1] treatments for many illnesses, including cancer. And if any part of your body is not healthy, you can "grow" a new one in a **laboratory**.

10   As you get dressed, you say to your shirt, "Turn red." It becomes red. In 2035, "smart clothes" contain nanoparticles that carry **electricity**. So you can **program** clothes to change colors or patterns.

On the way to the kitchen, you want to call a friend. Your
15   cell phone is by the window because the material it's made of takes in energy from the sun. But you don't need to pick up the phone. You can just touch your jacket sleeve[2] to make the call.

These are just some examples of nanotechnology all around you. "Your whole body and **surroundings** [will] become part of
20   the same network,"[3] says scientist Ampy Buchholz.

It's breakfast time. You reach for the milk, but a voice says, "Don't drink that!" Your fridge is reading a computer chip[4] on the milk. Every item from the **grocery** has a chip. Your fridge knows the milk is old, and tells the store you need new milk.

25   Finally, it's time to go to work. In 2035, cars drive themselves. Just tell your "smart car" where to go, and soon you will be there.

So, will all these predictions come true? Perhaps the future is much closer than we think.

With pieces of wearable technology like Google's smart contact lens on the way to becoming part of people's daily lives, perhaps the future is not so far away.

1   **Nanotechnology** is the science of very small things that are measured in nanometers (one billionth of a meter).
2   The **sleeves** of a shirt or jacket are the parts that cover your arms.
3   A **network** is a set of computers that send information to each other.
4   A **computer chip** is a very small piece of electronic equipment.

Reading Comprehension

Multiple Choice. Choose the best answer for each question.

Gist

1. The passage is mainly about _____ .
   a. medical treatments of the future
   b. how future technology may affect our lives
   c. how people will work and have fun in the future

Detail

2. What does the writer say about aging in the future?
   a. Age 60 will not be thought of as old.
   b. People who are 150 will look like they are 60.
   c. People who are 60 can expect to live 150 more years.

Vocabulary

3. In line 11, the word *smart* means _____ .
   a. nice-looking
   b. good at learning
   c. with a computer

Reference

4. The word *it's* (line 15) refers to _____ .
   a. the window
   b. the cell phone
   c. the sun

Detail

5. Which of the following predictions is NOT mentioned in the passage?
   a. You will be able to grow new body parts.
   b. Clothes will be able to change their patterns.
   c. There will be no more cell phones.

Inference

6. Which statement would Ampy Buchholz probably agree with?
   a. Nanotechnology will become very common in the future.
   b. Nano-sized particles may be dangerous to people's health.
   c. Life will be less interesting because everyone will look the same.

Did You Know?

A human hair is about 100,000 nanometers wide.

Understanding Prefixes and Suffixes

Prefixes (e.g., *un-, dis-, mis-*) are found at the beginning of words, and suffixes (e.g., *-al, -ly, -istic*) at the end of words. Knowing the meaning of prefixes and suffixes can help you understand new words and help build your vocabulary.

A. Completion. Look at the prefixes, meanings, and examples. Write a new word for each prefix using words from the box.

act   paid   national

∧ This pacemaker, a little machine that is put in a person's chest to help control their heart rhythms, is another example of how technology has changed our lives.

	Prefix	Meanings	Examples	Your ideas:
1.	re-	again/back to	return	_____
2.	inter-	between/among	Internet	_____
3.	pre-	before	predict	_____

B. Completion. Look at the suffixes, meanings, and examples. Write a new word for each suffix using words from the box.

pain   assess   invent

	Suffix	Meanings	Examples	Your ideas:
1.	-ful	full of	careful	_____
2.	-ment	act or manner	enjoyment	_____
3.	-ion	act or process	action	_____

C. Definitions. Find words in the first two paragraphs of the passage on page 169 containing these words. Write the word with its prefix or suffix. Then write a definition.

	Word	Word + prefix or suffix	Definition
1.	aging	_____	_____
2.	treat	_____	_____
3.	youth	_____	_____

Critical Thinking Discuss with a partner. Which of the predictions in the reading do you think will happen? Make a prediction about future technology. Does your partner agree?

Vocabulary Practice

A. Definitions. Use the words in the box to complete the definitions.

electricity	future	grocery	laboratory
mirror	program	surroundings	treatment

1. If you look into a(n) _____ , you see yourself.

2. A(n) _____ store sells different kinds of food.

3. Your _____ are the places, conditions, and things around you.

4. A(n) _____ is a room full of equipment where scientists work.

5. After you receive _____ for an illness, you usually look or feel better.

6. You _____ a machine by giving it instructions so it performs an action.

7. The _____ is the period of time that will happen after the present time.

8. _____ is energy that travels through wires and is used to operate machines.

B. Completion. Complete the information using words from the box in **A**.

Science fiction writers have long dreamed of cyborgs—people who have machines as body parts. Now that dream is a reality. Scientists have discovered ways to **1.** _____ machines to pick up signals from the brain, so people can operate them just by thinking.

After she lost her arm in a car accident, it was difficult for Amanda Kitts to do the **2.** _____ shopping and other everyday activities. Now Amanda has a robotic arm.

This technology is still very new. Though it has been tested many times in a **3.** _____ , it needs to be tested with real people. It may not work for everyone. However, many believe it won't be too far into the **4.** _____ before scientists succeed in fully joining humans and machines.

∨ Amanda Kitts with her robotic arm

> **Word Partnership**
> Use **future** with: (*adj.*) **near** future, **distant** future, **bright** future; (*v.*) **predict** the future, **shape** the future, **face** the future.

VIEWING Deep-sea Robot

Before You Watch

Predict. Look at the picture and read the caption.
Then check (✓) the things below that you think ROPOS can do.

< The ocean covers more than 70 percent of the Earth's surface, but only about 5 percent of the world's oceans have been explored, and we know even less about the creatures that live in its depths.[1]

In 2010, scientists from more than 80 countries started a project called the Census[2] of Marine[3] Life. They want to find out more about life in the ocean. It's a difficult project, but the scientists have help from a very special robot called ROPOS.

1 The **depths** of something refers to its deep places.
2 During a **census**, someone counts the number of people or animals in a place and gets information about them.
3 The term **marine** refers to anything to do with the ocean.

☐ record videos
☐ walk on land
☐ measure things
☐ cut things

☐ record sound
☐ take photos
☐ identify species
☐ help divers breathe

☐ pick up small animals
☐ suck up things
☐ think for itself
☐ dig in the ocean floor

While You Watch

Checking. As you watch the video, check your answers in **Before You Watch**. Were your ideas correct?

After You Watch

A. Multiple Choice. Choose the correct answer for each question below.

1. Why do the scientists use ROPOS to help them study deep-sea life?

   a. It is too dark in the deep water for humans to see.

   b. There are places too deep in the sea for humans to breathe.

   c. Sea animals are scared of people but not of ROPOS.

2. ROPOS can go _____ meters down into the ocean.

   a. 260   b. 2,600   c. 26,000

3. The video says ROPOS is the scientists' _____.

   a. eyes and ears   b. arms and legs   c. hands and feet

4. What does ROPOS stand for?

   a. Research Organism for Placement Of Sea Life

   b. Robotic Ocean Performance for Optical Study

   c. Remotely Operated Platform for Ocean Science

B. Matching. Match each of the following ideas from the video with their supporting details.

1. ____ We don't know much about our oceans.
2. ____ Scientists want to know more.
3. ____ A scientist says he can do things with ROPOS that he couldn't do before.
4. ____ ROPOS is a very well-equipped robot.
5. ____ ROPOS helps us understand more about deep-ocean life.

a. Many marine species are not known.

b. ROPOS has tools to cut, suck up, and dig.

c. Researchers have started the Census of Marine Life.

d. ROPOS helps the scientists see animals in their natural homes.

e. He can study animals in deep water as he could if they were found on land.

C. Discuss. Discuss these questions with a partner.

1. Do you think it's possible for humans to explore the whole ocean? Why or why not?

2. Do you think it's more important for humans to know about plants and animals in the ocean or on land?

Subarctic sunflower stars

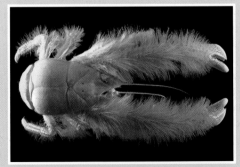

A yeti crab

< These sunflower stars and the yeti crab are some examples of species discovered by the Marine Census.

Photo Credits

Illustration Credits

29 (tr), 33 (c), 37 (cr), 57 (cr), 107 (cr), 125 (cr) National Geographic, 79 (br) National Geographic Maps

Text Credits

9 Adapted from "UFO Mystery," by Elisabeth Deffner: NGK, Mar 2008, 15 Adapted from "Unsolved Mystery: Atlantis," by Michael N. Smith and Debora L. Smith: NGK, Mar 2005, 23 Adapted from "A Slice of History," by Susan E. Goodman: NGE, 2005, 29 Adapted from "Hot Pod," by Catherine L. Barker: NGM, May 2007, 37 Adapted from "Grin and Bear it," by Russell Chadwick: NG World, Feb 2001, 42 Adapted from "An interview with Joel Sartore," by Joel Sartore: adapted from interviews from www.joelsartore.com, 51 Adapted from "Why is the *Titanic* Vanishing?," by Robert D. Ballard: NGM, Dec 2004, 57 Adapted from "Diamond Shipwreck," by Roff Smith: NGM, Nov 2009, 65 Adapted from "On the Case," by Dana Jensen and Natasha Metzler: NGE, Oct 2008, 71 Adapted from "Disease Detective," by Marylou Tousignant: NGE, Mar 2010, 79 Adapted from "Who was Sacagawea?," by Dana Jensen: NGE, Mar 2007, and "Searching for Sacagawea," by Margaret Talbot: NGM, Feb 2003, 84 Adapted from "Arctic Adventurer," by Dolores Johnson: NG Extreme Explorer, Jan-Feb 2010, 93 Adapted from "How to Decode Your Dreams," by Sarah Wassner: NGK, Aug 2005, and "Does Inception Tell the Truth About Dreams?," by Shalini Ramachandran, 98 Adapted from "Optical Illusions: NGE, Apr 2005, 107 Adapted from "Destination Antarctica: Emperor Penguins," by Crispin Boyer: NGK, Apr 2009, "Emperor Penguin: NG Website (http://animals.nationalgeographic.com/animals/birds/emperor-penguin/), "Penguins March On," by Jennifer Peters: NGE, Nov-Dec 2005, "Trapped by Ice," by Ruth Musgrave: NGK, Jan-Feb 2003, and "Happy Feet," by Deborah Underwood: NGK, Nov 2006, 113 Adapted from "What's So Funny?," by Aline Alexander Newman: NGK, Apr 2006, 121 Adapted from "Taj Mahal: NG Website (http://travel.nationalgeographic.com/travel/world-heritage/taj-mahal/), 126 Adapted from "Brunelleschi's Dome," by Tom Mueller: NGM, Feb 2014; 135 Adapted from "Weather Gone Wild," by Peter Miller: NGM, Sep 2012, 141 Adapted from "Ten Freaky Forces of Nature," by Douglas E. Richards: NGK, Sep 2008, 149 Adapted from "Mystery of the Frozen Mammoth," by Kristin Baird Rattini: NGK, May 2009; and "Ice Baby," by Tom Mueller: NGM, May 2009, 154 Adapted from "Sea Monster: NGE, Mar 2006, and "When Monsters Ruled the Deep," by Virginia Morell: NGM, Dec 2005, 163 Adapted from "Robot Revolution," by Douglas E. Richards: NGK, Feb 2008, "Robot World," by Sean Price: NGK, Jan-Feb 2003, and "Robots," by Chris Carroll: NGM, Aug 2011, 169 Adapted from "It's 2035," by Ruth Musgrave: NGK, Sep 2005, "Nanotechnology: Nano's Big Future," by Jennifer Kahn: NGM, June 2006, and "The Big Idea: Organ Regeneration," by Josie Glausiusz: NGM, Mar 2011

NGM = National Geographic Magazine, NGK = National Geographic Kids Magazine, NGE = National Geographic Explorer Magazine

Acknowledgments

The Authors and Publisher would like to thank the following teaching professionals for their valuable feedback during the development of this series:

Ahmed Mohamed Motala, University of Sharjah; **Ana Laura Gandini**, Richard Anderson School; **Andrew T. Om**, YBM PINE R&D; **Dr. Asmaa Awad**, University of Sharjah; **Atsuko Takase**, Kinki University, Osaka; **Bogdan Pavliy**, Toyama University of International Studies; **Brigitte Maronde**, Harold Washington College, Chicago; **Bunleap Heap**, American Intercon Institute; **Carey Bray**, Columbus State University; **Carmella Lieske**, Shimane University; **Chanmakara Hok**, American Intercon Institute; **Choppie Tsann Tsang Yang**, National Taipei University; **Cynthia Ross**, State College of Florida; **David Schneer**, ACS International, Singapore; **Dawn Shimura**, St. Norbert College; **David Barrett**, Goldenwest College, CA; **Dax Thomas**, Keio University; **Deborah E. Wilson**, American University of Sharjah; **Elizabeth Rodacker**, Bakersfield College; **Emma Tamaianu-Morita**, Akita University; **Fu-Dong Chiou**, National Taiwan University; **Gavin Young**, Iwate University; **George Galamba**, Woodland Community College; **Gigi Santos**, American Intercon Institute; **Gursharan Kandola**, Language and Culture Center, University of Houston, TX; **Heidi Bundschoks**, ITESM, Sinaloa Mexico; **Helen E. Roland**, ESL/FL Miami-Dade College-Kendall Campus; **Hiroyo Yoshida**, Toyo University; **Hisayo Murase**, Doshisha Women's College of Liberal Arts; **Ikuko Kashiwabara**, Osaka Electro-Communication University; **J. Lorne Spry**, Contracting University Lecturer; **Jamie Ahn**, English Coach, Seoul; **Jane Bergmann**, The University of Texas at San Antonio; **Jennie Farnell**, University of Connecticut; **José Olavo de Amorim**, Colegio Bandeirantes, Sao Paulo; **Kyoungnam Shon**, Avalon English; **Luningning C. Landingin**, American Intercon Institute; **Mae-Ran Park**, Pukyong National University, Busan; **Mai Minh Tiên**, Vietnam Australia International School; **Marina Gonzalez**, Instituto Universitario de Lenguas Modernas Pte., Buenos Aires; **Mark Rau**, American River College, Sacramento CA; **Max Heineck**, Academic Coordinator/Lecturer, King Fahd University of Petroleum & Minerals; **Dr. Melanie Gobert**, Higher Colleges of Technology; **Michael C. Cheng**, National Chengchi University; **Michael Johnson**, Muroran Institute of Technology; **Michael McGuire**, Kansai Gaidai University; **Muriel Fujii**, University of Hawaii; **Patrick Kiernan**, Meiji University; **Philip Suthons**, Aichi Shukutoku University; **Renata Bobakova**, English Programs for Internationals, Columbia, SC; **Rhonda Tolhurst**, Kanazawa University; **Rodney Johnson**, Kansai Gaidai University; **Rosa Enilda Vásquez Fernandez**, John F. Kennedy Institute of Languages, Inc.; **Sandra Kern**, New Teacher Coach, School District of Philadelphia; **Shaofang Wu**, National Cheng Kung University; **Sovathey Tim**, American Intercon Institute; **Stephen Shrader**, Notre Dame Seishin Women's University; **Sudeepa Gulati**, Long Beach City College; **Susan Orias**, Broward College; **Thays Ladosky**, Colegio Damas, Recife; **Thea Chan**, American Intercon Institute; **Tom Justice**, North Shore Community College; **Tony J.C. Carnerie**, UCSD English Language Institute; **Tsung-Yuan Hsiao**, National Taiwan Ocean University, Keelung; **Virginia Christopher**, University of Calgary-Qatar; **Vuthy Lorn**, American Intercon Institute; **Wm Troy Tucker**, Edison State College; **Yohei Murayama**, Kagoshima University; **Yoko Sakurai**, Aichi University; **Yoko Sato**, Tokyo University of Agriculture and Technology